George Miller Beard

Psychology Of The Salem Witchcraft Excitement

George Miller Beard

Psychology Of The Salem Witchcraft Excitement

ISBN/EAN: 9783741150395

Manufactured in Europe, USA, Canada, Australia, Japa

Cover: Foto ©berggeist007 / pixelio.de

Manufactured and distributed by brebook publishing software (www.brebook.com)

George Miller Beard

Psychology Of The Salem Witchcraft Excitement

THE
PSYCHOLOGY
OF THE
SALEM WITCHCRAFT EXCITEMENT
OF
1692

AND ITS PRACTICAL APPLICATION TO OUR OWN TIME

BY

GEORGE M. BEARD, A.M., M.D.

MEMBER OF THE NEW YORK NEUROLOGICAL SOCIETY, OF THE AMERICAN
NEUROLOGICAL ASSOCIATION, ETC.; AUTHOR OF NEURASTHENIA
(NERVOUS EXHAUSTION) AMERICAN NERVOUSNESS, ETC.

NEW YORK
G. P. PUTNAM'S SONS
27 AND 29 WEST 23D STREET
1882

RELATION OF SCIENCE

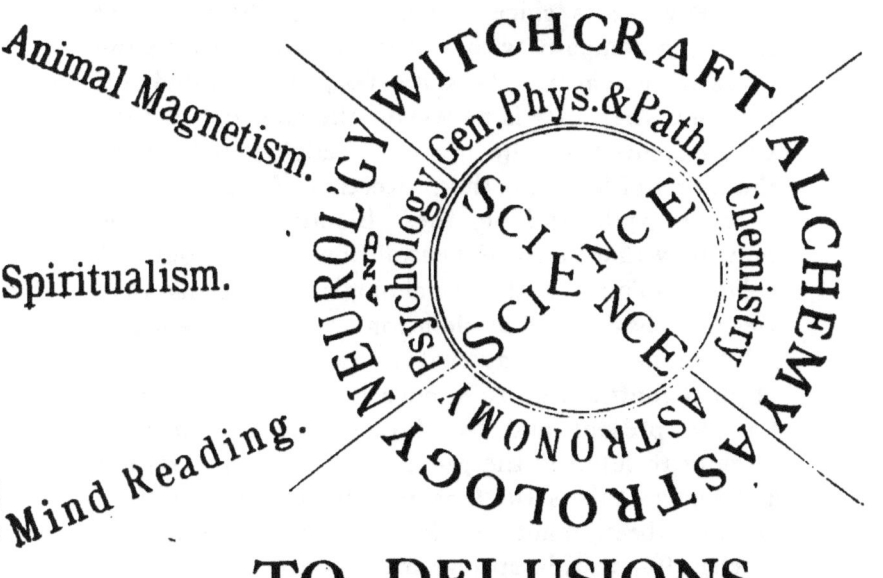

TO DELUSIONS.

(For Explanation See Appendix A.)

PREFACE.

A FEW years since, I was walking the streets of Salem, in company with a friend who showed me the relics of witchcraft days in 1692, and pointed out the spot where—as is believed—the innocent victims were executed—in the name of religion and under the forms of law—for the protection of society.

It was while studying these bloody object lessons of history that I formed a resolution to search out and solve, if might be, the psychological problems that were the basis of that delusion; and to present the solution in such a way that it should be at once an original contribution to science and a practical guide for the present and the future. This promise I attempt to fulfill in the present treatise, and—so far as I know—this is the first systematic attempt that has ever been made to lift the general subject of witchcraft—or this special manifestation of it—out of narrative and tradition into the science of psychology; for although now, for nearly two centuries, this country has been on its knees in repentance for what was done in Salem during this cyclone of fanaticism; and while a large and special and most interesting literature has grown up around those conscientious and ferocious procedures, yet, to no one of psychological training apparently has there come the thought that there was here a mine of psychology from which ore of high value could be obtained, which should be brought out milled and stamped in the name of science and humanity.

In the writings of Lecky, of Hutchinson, of Cotton Mather, of Calef, of Upham, of Poole and of Mudge, from which mainly the facts relating to the Salem witchcraft excitement are derived, we shall find no solution and no attempt at a solution of the phenomena, and scarcely a hint that such a solution is called for or would be welcomed. Science is beginning, however, to look in this direction. A series of papers on witchcraft by Dàvid Nicholson are being published in the *Journal of Mental Science*, during the present year. Just as the work is going to the press Mrs. Erminnie Smith, of Jersey City, N. J., a member of the New York Academy of Sciences, is preparing a report on sorcery among the Iroquois Indians, a subject that she has had and has improved unusual opportunities for studying.

Even Mr. Lecky—the best and most philosophical of all the writers on witchcraft, whose chapter on that subject in his " History of Rationalism," is the best contribution to its literature—has no explanation of its phenomena beyond the general fact of the untrustworthiness of human testimony; but he establishes very clearly that the delusion died out, gradually and —in the main—quietly, as the result of the general advance of the human mind, rather than of any interpretation of the mystery. Mr. Lecky, however, is enough in advance of all other writers on this subject to see that a scientific study of this subject is demanded, and in a most remarkable passage in his " History of Morals" (p. 167, Am. ed.), he asserts that the bringing of these and allied phenomena into science is one of the world's greatest and most pressing problems.

Great trials of this kind are landmarks of human non-expertness, measures of the cerebral force of nations; they tell us how low we stand, how slowly we advance; they are educators of the future, and may most wisely be studied, in scientific detail, by the psychologist and philosopher.

There are times in the evolution of delusions, and in the history of nations—in which delusions are organized—when non-expertness in any special line— long restrained through circumstances or negligence— becomes a volcano; the low mutterings and reverberations that are at once so frequent and so slight, but so harmless as to cause no alarm, suddenly cease, and from the long quiet crater an eruption appears, darkening the sky and burying the earth in its fiery streams. Such was the witchcraft excitement in Salem in 1692; such was the Guiteau excitement in Washington, in 1882; the one marking the death of the dogma that the innocent should be condemned to death for the fancied crime of witchcraft, on spectre-evidence; and the other marking the death of the dogma that ability to know right from wrong is proof of responsibility, and that the insane who commit murder should be hanged.

As the twenty victims of the Salem judicial massacres were nearly the last of the immense army of murdered witches, so Guiteau will be nearly the last important lunatic ever hanged on this continent; and through all time his trial will stand—as the Salem Witchcraft trials have stood—as a historic memorial of the power of passion reinforced by superstition.

The researches, the results of which are given in these pages, have occupied at intervals a number of years. Their publication at this time is especially appropriate, on account of the increasing frequency with which questions relating to the judicial treatment of insanity and allied states are coming before the courts and the people. Two important trials, with which from first to last I was professionally connected, that of Cadet Whittaker and that of Guiteau, have impressed on many minds besides my own the need of a study and a re-study of psychology both in its scientific and its political relations. The parallelism between the Salem witchcraft trials and the trial of Guiteau is especially instructive, and, as the two excitements throw light on each other, the case of Guiteau is often referred to in this treatise.

Our country is indeed just now passing through an epidemic similar to that of Salem, though in a milder and modified form. Guiteau, as is shown in these pages, is in one sense the successor of the victims of witchcraft; the scenes of Salem have been in a degree repeated in Washington. This attempt of the nineteenth century to duplicate the non-expertness of the seventeenth has succeeded only in part, and for a brief period; and it is pleasing to be able to say that this comparative study of these two mental epidemics—that of 1692, and that of 1882—gives on the whole potent encouragement to those who believe and hope for progress of the nation and the race.

The substance of this work was first presented in the form of a lecture with experiments—a kind of moot court— after the manner of the trials at Salem, before the New York Academy of Sciences, April 3, 1882. The experiments, illustrating spectre testimony, were made on two of my trance subjects on whom I had previously experimented and whom I knew to be genuine. One of these young men, while in artificial trance, became violently convulsed, when brought near to the supposed witch, and fell on the floor; and the other saw spectres of ravens over or near the witch's head. That these young men were really entranced had been clearly established by numerous experiments of various kinds made by myself and by others; but, as I distinctly pointed out in the lecture, it was of no significance practically whether their trances were genuine or feigned ; in either case the spectres and convulsions were worthless as evidence; but on just such testimony—whether real or assumed—our fathers in Salem tried, convicted, and murdered their neighbors and friends.

In the study of the case of Guiteau, I had the opportunity of a number of interviews with the prisoner ; listened to some of his testimony on the stand, and also to that of a number of other witnesses. I attended for a short time one of those extraordinary and incredible caucuses of experts, in which it was conscientiously hoped that, by a comparison of views, a substantial agreement could be reached ; whereas the independent, unbiased, and original opinion of the expert, without reference to the opinion of any other human being—there or elsewhere—was what was needed on that trial. In the study of the case of Guiteau, I was much aided by an analysis and comparison of a number of cases of monomania much resembling his, that are or have been under my professional care. The best literature of the subject—I may be allowed to add—is the older French literature, the writings of Esquirol and Pinel. In connection with these may be consulted a few German writers: Casper, Eminghaus, and Krafft-Ebing, and others. The English and American literature of insanity has tended to bring confusion rather than clearness and consistency, and is to be avoided by those who are seeking for light, especially on that form of insanity known as monomania.

The necessity for a reconstruction of ideas in regard to insanity, on the basis of evolution, has been made apparent by recent cases, as that of Guiteau and McLean; and I may add, also, of a number of other cases, like that of Lamson, where the plea of insanity was presented without good reason.

Not being in Washington at the time when the experts first began to testify for the defence, I was not sent for; but at a later date, in response to a telegram, I returned to Washington, and went on the stand, prepared to answer for the defence the hypothetical questions of the prosecution relating to the symptoms of insanity manifested by Guiteau. My testimony was to have been introduced by way of rebuttal, and, on legal grounds was ruled out by the Judge. The testimony that I was then prepared to give, was, in substance, that which I had given in the *North American Review*, which I have since given in my paper on the case of Guiteau, and which is now again presented in this treatise.

My conclusions in regard to the trial of Cadet Whittaker of the West Point Military Academy, were the result of careful and prolonged study. I had the advantage of a number of interviews with Whittaker, and made many experiments on him, the especial purpose of which he has never known, and could not suspect. I found him to be of a shrinking, yielding, timid and most conscientious temperament, with very far less than average of mental and muscular control, the last person to remain motionless and calm, *with perfectly normal pulse*, under circumstances, the most trying in which a human being could be placed. The mere excitement of coming to see me sent his pulse to one hundred; in the second visit it was eighty, and not until I had seen him several times did I find that his natural pulse was somewhat slow—sixty-eight to seventy—and this was his pulse when found unconscious and prostrate in his room at West Point. The report of the surgeon of the Post, Dr. Alexander, is a classical description of the sleep that follows unconsciousness from fright, and of the usual phenomena when aroused. But as in Salem, Dr. Griggs mistook the symptoms of hysteria and trance for possession of the devil, and so started the witchcraft murders, so Dr. Alexander mistook the symptoms of trance for shamming, an error into which a conscientious non-expert in psychology might easily have fallen.

The Court of Inquiry at West Point was conducted closely after the model of the Salem trials, the guilt of the accused being assumed, and the proofs of innocence being interpreted as proofs of guilt; hence the unexampled conduct of General Schofield for which he was properly removed from his position; hence the prolonged court-martial in New York, asked for by Whittaker and granted by President Hayes. The members of the Court of Inquiry and the members of the court-martial voted at the end of the trials as they would have voted at the beginning, without consideration of the evidence on either side. Having been connected with the case all through the court-martial, and having made myself familiar with all the hand-writing and other testimony, I am able to say that there was no more evidence that Whittaker cut his own ears and feigned unconsciousness than there was that our fathers and mothers in Salem were witches.

The protracted illness of President Garfield, by causing delay in reviving the Whittaker case, kept the nation from confirming the unjust decision of the court-martial; the storm of passion had passed by; the awful form of Guiteau filled the stage; the country was no longer angry against Whittaker; a national sorrow saved us from a national disgrace.

Those who fear that my condemnation of spectral hand-writing testimony by which Whittaker was condemned is too strong, will find on page 373 of Sergeant Ballantine experiences (just published), these words: " Hand-writing is a dangerous element upon which to rest a case ; the evidence of what are called experts is viewed with no great confidence. Jurors distrust it." I am sure that no jury in the world would ever have convicted Whittaker. The late surrogate of New York, Hon. Delano C. Calvin, very recently expressed to me a similar opinion of hand-writing testimony, observing furthermore that, unlike experts in other branches, hand-writing experts have no standard work to which they can appeal; all is a matter of individual experience or feeling.

Some of the topics referred to in this work are discussed in more detail in other writings, of which I may mention the following:

The Case of Guiteau, a psychological study, in the *Journal of Mental and Nervous Disease*, January, 1882; The study of Trance and Muscle-Reading and Allied Nervous Phenomena ; my monograph on " The Nature and Phenomena of Trance," or, The Scientific Basis of Delusions; papers on " Experiments with Human Beings," and on the "Scientific Study of Human Testimony," in the *Popular Science Monthly*. In a paper on " The Psychology of Spiritualism," in the *North American Review*, July, 1879, and January, 1882, I gave a resumé of these and related topics.

PREFACE. xv

One of the most interesting of the many psychological facts brought out by this investigation is the readiness with which nations sometimes approve and applaud crimes of other nations which they would not themselves dare to commit. England is America beyond the sea, the real republic of Europe; the two nations differing chiefly in age, the one in its wooden, the other in its brazen decade; both inhabited mostly by Philistines. England, in 1692, would not have executed twenty of her citizens for witchcraft, although it was a crime she had herself helped to create; and the Salem trials and executions were based on English laws and English decisions; but through some of her representatives she complimented New England on her zeal for God and the protection of society. England in 1882 would not have convicted or even tried Guiteau, although both trial and conviction were made possible only by English precedents; but she said amen and amen to the verdict at Washington. Meantime her own Guiteau,—McLean, excited not unlikely by the example of the murderer of Garfield, assaulted the Queen, and was quickly sent to an asylum at Her Majesty's pleasure, on proofs of insanity only fractionally as strong as the proofs of the insanity of Guiteau. No other nation would have convicted Guiteau; no other nation would have tried him, but other nations for the moment rejoiced to hear that the young and haughty republic could convict a lunatic of political crime.

The cessation of the Salem slaughters was followed by long discussions that even yet are in full activity, as to due apportionment of the disgrace. The clergy censured the lawyers, the lawyers the clergy, or each other; the people blamed their leaders, but the leaders could not well blame the people, who had applauded their deeds, for all had been done logically, scripturally, conscientiously, for the glory of God, the protection of society and the general welfare of man.

Similarly the disgrace of the trial and conviction of the insane Guiteau cannot be exclusively appropriated by any one man or any one class. The remarkable judge, who, sitting on the most famous trial of the century, thought it to be his duty, like the jurymen, to abstain from reading and informing himself on insanity, lest his mind should be biased in the direction of justice, and who at last threw into his charge the chips of science and the leavings of law; the jury who, as some of them have since disclosed, sat down to the trial as an idle form, and rendered the verdict without reference to testimony for prosecution or defence; the counsel who consulted and exchanged epithets with the irresponsible prisoner; the press, that with unanimity—almost absolute—fell on its knees before its patrons, and took counsel of violence rather than of science as to what it should say;* the pulpit that substantially republished the sermons of Salem; the court in banc that reaffirmed the unspeakable dogma that a knowledge of right and wrong is a test of responsibility; the physicians who, with exceptions very few, were too late in presenting the truths of psychology, and some of whom, by previous agreement, testified that insanity was not hereditary, and that the symptoms of insanity were really the symptoms of sanity—all these must share in the most dreadful event of its kind that has darkened our history for two hundred years.

If to any one class should be assigned a medal for special and peculiar and overshadowing non-expertness, it must be, as is usual in such cases, to the lawyers, who in Salem both led the trials and long after contended for the logic by which they were held, and in Washington dared not defend the most defenceless of prisoners. Years hence, when emotion has given way to reason, and the trial at Washington

---

* In the above strictures on the press exception should be made in favor of the *North American Review*. That bold and powerful magazine, at an early stage, when the storm was thickest, even before the trial, ventured on the experiment of asking experts on the nervous system to express their opinions on the question of the moral responsibility of the insane, at the risk that some of them might tell the truth in regard to Guiteau. It is doubtful whether the contribution which I made to that symposium would have been published by any other lay journal in our language.

has taken its place side by side with the trials in Salem, in the permanent record of judicial cruelty and non-expertness, some philosophic historian, in the light of a purer science, and gifted with a higher pre-science and keener vision than any of us to-day, shall note that of the physicians a few were from the first prepared to testify, and in and out of court did testify against the crime of arraigning one who could so commit no crime—but must also note that among the lawyers there was not one of eminence in all the land to do for Guiteau what Erskine did for Hadfield, what Seward did for the negro Freeman,* and take the side of science against delusions in the face of a mob of non-experts fifty millions strong.

"The conduct of Mr. Seward, in undertaking the defence of Freeman, when he was arraigned for the

* The negro, William Freeman, had murdered a whole family, including Mr. John G. Van Nest, an aged and respectable farmer, his wife, and an infant, and had injured others. He stole a horse and escaped; stabbed the animal, then stole another, continued his flight, and was captured forty miles from the scene of the murders. He was tried in Auburn, N. Y., July, 1846.

The above is taken from Snyder's volume "Great Speeches by Great Lawyers," pp. 149, *et seq.* Students of the legal relations of insanity will do wisely to read the whole speech, in connection with that of Erskine for Hadfield (see Erskine's speeches).

Dr. Spitzka, in an important paper read before the New York Medico Legal Society, May 3, 1882, made a pertinent reference to the case of William Freeman.

murder, was an exhibition of moral courage almost without a parallel. The crime charged was terrible and appalling, and wrought upon the public mind to such a degree it was almost a miracle how the prisoner escaped swift destruction at the hands of a mob. He was without money and without friends. He sprung from a race socially and politically debased. His father had been a slave, and the son was a person of idle and intemperate habits, and, though only twenty-three, had spent five years of his life in the State prison. Yet Mr. Seward was convinced that the poor wretch was, at the time of the offence, destitute of reason, and suffering from dementia approaching to idiocy. He believed the execution of such a being would be murder, and he determined to spare the community the disgrace of hanging a madman, even at the cost of his own popularity. The storm of public indignation beat so fiercely about him, that at one time fears were entertained for his personal safety." In a letter to a friend he thus referred to the subject : " There is a busy war around me to drive me from securing a fair trial for the negro Freeman. . . . No priest (except one Universalist), no Levite, no lawyer, no man, no woman, has visited him. He is deaf, deserted, ignorant, and his conduct is unexplainable on any principle of *sanity*. It is natural he should turn to me to defend him. If he does, I shall do so. This will raise a storm of prejudice and passion which will try the fortitude of my friends. But I shall do my duty. I care not whether I am to be ever forgiven for it or not."

"John Van Buren, Attorney-General, closed the case for the people, and the Hon. Bowen Whiting delivered the charge. The Jury, after consultation on the 23d July, returned a verdict of guilty, and the prisoner was, at 6.30 o'clock the next morning, sentenced to be hanged on the 18th September. Mr. Seward obtained a writ of error, and the conviction was afterward reversed and a new trial ordered. (Freeman v. The People, 4 Denio.) After a reversal of the General Term, the prisoner was visited by the Circuit Judge with reference to the propriety of having arraigned him, and it is said he declined to try him again. The prisoner died in his cell August 21st, 1847. A post-mortem examination was had, which revealed the fact that his brain had been long diseased, and that he must have been insane before the murder."

The future will read the case of Guiteau, and the case of Whittaker, as we now read the case of Freeman and the witchcraft trials of Salem.

GEO. M. BEARD.

NEW YORK, 52 West 34th, June 10, 1882.

THE PSYCHOLOGY

OF

SALEM WITCHCRAFT.

CHAPTER I.

THE new world, from the time of its settlement, has been a kind of health resort for the worn-out delusions of the old. Erroneous beliefs, starving for want of pasture in Europe, their lungs gone or going, thinned to skeletons, transplanted, like consumptives, to those milder shores, are made alive again, and renew somewhat of their power to degrade and destroy. For years prior to the Salem excitement, European witchcraft had been prostrate on its dying bed, under the watchful and apprehensive eyes of religion and of law; carried over the ocean it arose to its feet, and threatened to depopulate New England; but, as often with exiled invalids, its recovery was transient and unnatural; the Salem murders were its last deeds of blood, and soon it was quietly buried, without the pomp of a funeral, under the very soil where it was hoped it had found the elixir of eternity. In crossing the Atlantic, sea-gulls follow the steamer for long distances that they may feed on the floating refuse; so America has followed and fed on the cast-off philosophies and forgotten cruelties of Europe, and has been grateful for the privilege, our non-expert judges often contending who should be the first to seize the ignoble prize.*

The number of persons executed in New England for witchcraft was comparatively very small. According to Mr. Poole, but thirty-two were killed; twenty during the Salem excitement, and twelve at different times and places preceding the great excitement—the first case being in 1648; whereas, in Europe, in a century or two preceding, there had been probably half a million executions under the same delusion.

It was not, therefore, the number of those slain in Salem in 1692 that has given to that time and that place a special, powerful, and terrible immortality; but because it was the last act in the long tragedy of terror and blood. It is only or mainly when delu-

* During the last decade the relation of the two continents in this respect has been in some directions reversed; the delusions of Spiritualism, of Animal Magnetism, and more recently of Mind Reading, after having been exposed and shorn of their force in America, have been welcomed in England as revelations by members of the Royal Society and the royal family, by the University of Leipsic, and not a few philosophers of France and Germany.

sions are dying that they arouse important attention ; a belief that everybody believes—that is the common breath of society—is assumed, like the darkness of night, and calls out no comment and no thought, and may fill no serious or important place in history. The Salem murders were the last struggles, the death-rattle of the monster that had been wandering for centuries wild over Europe.

Active convulsions are signs not of strength but of debility, and are often the immediate precursors of death ; a body of matter impinging against the earth's atmosphere suddenly becomes a meteor, and rushes to its quick destruction with a great sound and flame ; meantime its starry comrades revolve in silence and unseen : through long decades, even through centuries, a tree may stand obscure, but when it falls the whole forest, as has been said, resounds with the noise of its fall. The death of a delusion, like the death of a man, draws more notice than its life, and if it be violent the world stops its noisy tread to gaze upon it.

SALEM MURDERS THOUGHT TO BE NECESSARY FOR THE PROTECTION OF SOCIETY.

In the Salem trials, as in the Guiteau trial, the magistrates and the people were laboring, as they thought, for the protection of society in Salem ; they felt as sure that their neighbors and friends were in league with the devil, as we have felt that Guiteau was the murderer of President Garfield; and to our ancestors, the crime of being in league with the devil was a greater crime than murder. With the Zunis Indians, some of whose chiefs have lately visited the Eastern States, witchcraft is the only crime that is punished with death; and they expressed an interest, as I am told, in the history of the Salem horrors.

All delusions have their war-cry—some short, simple phrase borne on the wind, heard, and constantly repeated by all. The war-cry in Salem was, "He has an evil eye," or "evil hand;" the war-cry in Washington has been, "Sane enough to hang."

Before and during the Salem trials, the clergy and the politicians, the prominent citizens, conservators of public morals, united in the expression of the fear that they were becoming too lax, and easy and gentle in the treatment of witches; that the scriptural commands of murder were not enforced as rigidly as they should be, and that the nation was in peril for want of more shedding of blood. Before and during the Guiteau trial, the press and the people, the judges, the clergy, dropped other differences that they might agree in this, that we, as a people, were becoming too merciful toward murderers; that the plea of insanity was overused; and that those who were really crazy ought to be punished for their crimes, in order to elevate the public morals and save the republic; and it was felt, almost unanimously, that the lunatic Guiteau would be an excellent and valuable victim on which to illustrate the public desire to originate new methods of dealing with the insane.

The favorite text in Salem was, "Thou shalt not suffer a witch to live;" the favorite text in Washington was, "Whoso sheddeth man's blood, by man shall his blood be shed." In Salem, the lawyers, and the judges, and the great counselors of the day were of the first, after the clergy, to incite, and the last to repent of the shedding of blood; here, as always and everywhere, law being behind all other branches, and filling up the rear in the slow evolution of the race. In Salem, the doctors diagnosed the symptoms of insanity, hysteria, and trance as evidences of witchcraft; and when the bodies of the innocent men and delicate maidens were subjected to cruel tortures, the surgeons stood by, and gave advice and assistance. From beginning to end of the trials, no man of science, of any grade, seems to have raised a voice for science.

On the Guiteau trial, specialists in the nervous system testified, others were ready to testify, and, under right management of the defense, would have testified that the prisoner was insane; and, during the long trial, no high authority on the nervous system was found to testify to the contrary. This contrast in the courage and knowledge of physicians marks the scientific advance of these two centuries.

THE TRIALS BASED ON OLD ENGLISH PRECEDENTS.

There are always precedents for injustice. In the Salem witchcraft trials the judges consulted—according to Cotton Mather—the following precedents, in condemning their neighbors, relatives, and friends to death:

"The Precepts laid down by learned Writers about Witchcraft, as, Keble on the Common Law, chap. 'Conjuration' (an author approved by the twelve judges of our nation!). Also, Sir Matthew Hale's 'Trials of Witches,' printed Anno 1682; Glanville's Collection of Sundry Trials in England and Ireland, in the years 1658, '61, '63, '64, and '81; Bernard's Guide to ' Janywing Baxter's and R. B. their Histories about Witches, and their Discoveries,' and Cotton Mather's 'Memorable Providences relating to Witchcraft,' printed 1685."

In 1664, Sir Matthew Hale sentenced two females to death for witchcraft, and thus gave sanction to the delusion. In the same century, King James of England wrote in favor of witchcraft; and Parliament, by cruel and bloody legislation, echoed his views and opinions. In the same century—which has been called the witchcraft century—physicians shouted *vive la* witchcraft; when they saw a case which baffled their skill, it was an all-comprehending plea for them to place it to the credit of possession of the devil—to say it was "the evil hand."

One Matthew Hopkins, in England, became so expert in detecting witches that he followed it as a legitimate profession; traveled under the sanction of government, which paid his expenses, and also allowed him a fee for each person who was convicted through his agency. He was known as the "Witch-finder General." He had power to torture, and used his power to such an extent that in one year three-score unfortunates died under his hand.

In Salem, Giles Corey died a horrible death—being crushed by a weight placed upon his breast—refusing to the last to plead himself guilty or not guilty of witchcraft. There was English precedent for pressing to death those who refused to plead—that is, to answer the question "Guilty or not guilty?"

The poet Longfellow puts these words into Cotton Mather's lips, as he looks upon Corey's dead and mangled body:

> "O sight most horrible! In a land like this,
> Spangled with churches evangelical,
> Inwrapped in our salvation, must we seek
> In moldering statute-books of English courts
> Some old forgotten law to do such deeds!
> Those who lie buried in the Potter's Field
> Will rise again, as surely as ourselves
> That sleep in honored graves with epitaphs,
> And this poor man, whom we have made a victim,
> Hereafter will be counted as a martyr."

WITCHCRAFT DEFINED.

Before the Salem witchcraft excitement, as well as since, there has been no definition of witchcraft; everybody believed in it, but nobody knew what it was; and to this day it has never been defined; and there is not, I believe, in any language a work on the subject that has value in science, or that was written by a man in any way competent to deal with it. "Witchcraft is the belief in the possession of the devil."

The indictments used in Salem on the 29th of February, 1692—the day that marks the judicial beginning of the excitement—against certain persons, named "Good," "Osburn," "Tituba," charged the prisoners with "certain detestable arts called witchcraft and sorceries, wickedly and feloniously used, practised and exercised," by which persons named —the so-called "afflicted children"— were "tortured, afflicted, fined, consumed, wasted, and tormented."

All this is vague and unscientific.

The leading idea all through witchcraft was that the devil entered into people; and that persons of high position and noted for piety sometimes entered into covenant with Satan to do evil work, such as tormenting or killing their neighbors and friends, or injuring the earth in many ways. It was claimed

THEORY OF WITCHCRAFT.

that the devil would appear as a "black man," or in any other shape he chose to assume; he presented a book and made a bargain with those who consented to act as his agents; and he, on his part, promised to confer upon his allies riches, eloquence, and strength, and bestow upon them amazing powers, and they could go to do his will in the form of a dog, a cat, a hog, mouse, or toad, or a bird. Such was the belief in Salem in 1692, the date of the excitement I am here analyzing.

It was a part of the theory of the witchcraft delusion that the devil used the spectres of some persons to affect other persons. Some contended that the devil could employ only the spectres of persons "who were in league with him;" others that he could employ the spectres of "innocent persons, without their knowledge or consent." The former idea—that he could only employ the spectres of persons who were in voluntary league with him—was the dogma on which the Salem tricks were founded, and the dogma which convicted all who were accused; just as the dogma of the ability to know right from wrong would condemn nearly every lunatic who is arraigned for murder.

In Salem village, the suspected witches, male and female, were subjected, as the custom for ages had been, to examination with pins, all over the body, in order to detect the shriveled and callous and nonsensitive places, which were supposed to be diagnostic of bewitchment. Some of these pins, preserved in one of the public buildings in Salem, I had the pleasure of seeing a few years ago. Mr. Upham, in his History of the Salem Witchcraft, makes this observation:

"Great ignorance prevailed in reference to the influence of the body and the mind upon each other. While the imagination was called into more extensive and energetic action than at any preceding period, its properties and laws were but little understood; the extent of the connection of the will and the muscular system, the reciprocal influence of the nerves and the fancy, and the strong and universally pervading healthy condition of physical and moral constitutions were almost wholly unknown. These important subjects are, indeed, but imperfectly understood, even at the present day."

These are true words; the very best words in Upham's work. If the involuntary life, the interactions of mind and body—including trance, muscle-reading, insanity, hysteria and allied nervous phenomena, had been understood as we understand gravity, chemistry, astronomy, and physics, there would have been no trials in Salem.

One of the favorite phases of withcraft in those days was a belief in imps. The imp was a familiar spirit that the witch sent out to do evil to others; the imp must, however, return to the witch for sustenance, from which it derived the power to injure and torment those to whom it was sent. The belief was, that spots on the body which, by the needle-test, were found to be numb, were the teats whence the imp derived sustenance. Suspected witches were watched night and day, in order to see these imps come and go, and holes were left in the door, through which they might enter and depart; and those who watched probably became entranced, and no doubt did see imps come and go: and on the strength of this kind of evidence the suspected witches were condemned and murdered.

Witches used to keep images of those persons whom they wished to torment; these images were made of cloth, hair, etc.; and by teasing and tormenting them, the persons whom they wished to afflict were teased, tormented, or burned; as though hanging a man in effigy were the same thing as hanging him in the original. There is no doubt that many persons charged with witchcraft became insane or entranced, and that while entranced or insane they did see these images or imps, confessed accordingly, and were—very logically—hanged therefor.

Any unusual marks—any callosities such as warts or wens, to which aged persons are liable—were regarded as signs of witchcraft, and persons suspected of being witches were searched by persons of the same sex, in order to find such marks. If any person were charged with having tormented another, it was useless for him to state—and bring proof of the statement—that he was a thousand miles away, at the time it occurred, for it was recognized that his spectre or apparition could do all that he could do, if personally present.

Witchcraft is the tragedy of humanity; says Mr. Lecky. " It is probable that no class of victims endured sufferings so unalloyed and so intense. Not for them the wild fanaticism that nerves the soul against danger, and almost steels the body against torments. Not for them the solace of lamenting friends, or the consciousness that their memories would be cherished and honored by posterity; they died alone, hated and unpitied."

Some of the witches were tortured into confessing; they were tied, neck and heels, until the blood was ready to come out from their noses; they were treated as at one time it was desired that Guiteau should be treated. It seems that it paid them to confess; for out of fifty-five who did confess none were hanged, except those who afterward recanted their confessions.

The prisoners, men and women—some of them persons of social position and property—were, for months, bound with cords and irons, outraged by unfeeling scrutiny, insulted on examinations, buried in wretched and crowded prisons, deprived of the comforts of association, and in every way distressed and annoyed, excommunicated from the church, and given over to the devil, whose agents they were supposed to be.

"If the witch was obdurate, the first and it was said the most effectual method of obtaining confession was by what was termed 'waking her.' An iron bridle or hoop was bound across her face, with four prongs which were thrust into her mouth. It was fastened behind to the wall by a chain in such a manner that the victim was unable to lie down; and in this position she was sometimes kept for several days, while men were constantly with her to prevent her closing her eyes for a moment in sleep. Partly in order to effect this purpose, and partly to discover the insensible mark which was the sure sign of a witch, long pins were thrust into her body. At the same time—as it was a saying in Scotland that a witch would never confess while she could drink—excessive thirst was added to her tortures. Some persons, it is said, have been waked five nights; one, it is said, even for nine."

"The physical and mental suffering of such a process was sufficient to overcome the resolution of many, and to distract the understanding of not a few. But other and perhaps worse tortures were in reserve. The three principal tortures that were habitually applied were the pennywinks, the boots, and the caschielawis. The first was a kind of thumbscrew; the second was a frame in which the leg was inserted, and where it was broken by wedges driven in by a hammer; the third was also an iron frame for the leg, which was from time to time heated over a brazier. Fire matches were sometimes applied to the body of the victim." "We read in a contemporary legal register of one man who was kept for forty-eight hours in 'vehement torture' in the caschielawis; and of another who remained in the same frightful machine for eleven days and eleven nights, whose legs were broken daily for fourteen days in the boots, and who was so scourged that the whole skin was torn from his body." To what extent all these historic methods of torture were used in Salem will never be known in detail.

ORIGIN AND EVOLUTION OF THE TRIALS—THE AFFLICTED CHILDREN.

The basis of the Salem witchcraft trials was composed of the complex phenomena of trance, insanity, and hysteria, and it was ignorance of the phenomena of trance, insanity, and hysteria that made those trials possible. The Salem horrors were the penalty of our ancestors' non-expertness in psychology.

TRANCE, HYSTERIA, AND INSANITY.

The specific origin of the Salem trials was the convening of a number of young girls, so-called "afflicted children," who, under the combined influence of wonderful stories appealing to the imagination, and mental contagion, became partly insane and partly entranced, partly hysterical; and, in that state, saw visions, spectres, apparitions, ghosts of murdered victims, demons, which visions were ascribed to certain individuals living near them. The phenomena of trance and hysteria and insanity were supplemented by not a little deviltry, and cruel, intentional crime, on the part, no doubt, of the victims, and of their neighbors.

The phenomena of trance, of hysteria, and of insanity in Salem were interpreted as the phenomena of witchcraft, and those whom the afflicted children accused were arrested, tried, and murdered.

The afflicted children—who were the chief accusers in all the excitements, and who constituted what we now call a spiritual séance—were Elizabeth, the daughter of Mr. Parrish, a girl about nine years of age; Abigail Williams, a niece of Mr. Parrish, a girl eleven years of age; Ann Putnam, twelve years of age; Mary Wolcott, seventeen years of age; Mary Lewis, a servant girl of Rev. Mr. Burroughs, seventeen years of age; Elizabeth Hubbard, aged seventeen, a niece of the wife of Dr. Griggs, the village physician, and a member of his family; Mary Warren, a servant in the Proctor family, aged about twenty years; and

Sarah Churchill, another servant ; these girls were reinforced by Mrs. Putnam, Mrs. Pope, a woman by the name of Bibber and another named Goodell. Out of such persons precisely, spiritual séances of the present generation are made; the higher intelligence of our time making it impossible for them to do any very serious evil beyond propagating insane fancies and bloodless delusions like animal magnetism, psychometry, or mind-reading.

In the meetings which this circle held, the members of it were thrown into convulsions, uttered loud cries, and professed to experience, and, no doubt, did experience, severe tortures and sufferings. Out of such a circle as this developed the spirit-rapping excitement at Rochester which was the modern evolution of witchcraft known as spiritualism ; in such circles the Eddy Brothers, in my presence, recently raised the dead, and Katie King appeared in human form. If this Salem circle of afflicted children had possessed the rapping power with joints that the Fox girls possessed ; if they could have read muscle like " Brown, the mind-reader," and his disciples ; if they could have achieved any of the slate-writing tricks of modern mediums, their power for evil would have been titanic. Some of these afflicted children—though not all—became in time abandoned ; thus demonstrating the frequent affinity—illustrated in all ages—of coarse immorality and coarse delusions.

After the "afflicted children," as they were called, had made some excitement, and Mr. Parris, the pastor, had found that he could not understand it, or make any satisfactory explanation of the trouble, Dr. Griggs, the town physician, was called in; and he, not being an expert in hysteria, trance, or insanity, gave the diagnosis of witchcraft, saying, "They have the evil eye."* The people very soon became convinced that there were witches among them; that is, persons in league with the devil, who by their apparitions were tormenting the children.

Bentley says: "The torrent of opinion was irresistible. They who thought they saw the delusion did not oppose it. They who were deluded were terrified into distraction."

The first charges were made against comparatively obscure and uninfluential persons; then by degrees individuals of prominence were charged; until at last the accusers struck too high, and the executions ceased.

---

* Margaret Jones, of Boston, was one of the victims of the witchcraft delusion in 1648. She used to cure by putting persons in artificial trance, and for that she was—very properly and logically—murdered.

Dr. James Oakes, a skillful physician of that day, being called in, made the diagnosis of "an evil hand, or evil eye."

Mr. Poole, from whose monograph I have obtained this fact, makes the following truthful and painful remark: "A skillful physician seems to be in the ground-plan of nearly every witchcraft case in New England."

The following took place in court, before Judge Hathorne, and illustrates the nature of the delusion, and its influence over even the learned and eminent men of that generation:

"'Sarah Good, what evil spirit have you familiarity with?'

"'None.'

"'Have you made no contracts with the devil?'

"'No.'

"'Why do you hurt these children?'

"'I do not hurt them. I scorn it.'

"'Who do you employ, then, to do it?'

"'I employ no one.'

"'What creature do you employ then?'

"'No creature, but I am falsely accused.'

"Judge Hathorne desired the children, all of them, to look upon her, and see if this were the person that hurt them, and so they did all look upon her, and said this was one of the persons that did torment them, and presently they were all tormented."

Her husband, even, was afraid that she was a witch, or would be one very quickly.

When Goody Nurse was tried, the following questions and answers appeared:

"Do you see," said Judge Hathorne, "what a solemn condition these are in? When your hands are loose these persons are afflicted." She answers: "The Lord knows I have not hurt them; I am an innocent person."

METHOD OF EXAMINATION.

Judge Hathorne replies: "It is very awful for all to see these agonies, and you, an old professor, thus charged with contracting with the devil by the effects of it, and yet to see you stand with dry eyes when there are so many wet." It was one of the doctrines of witchcraft that witches could not weep. The Judge said: "You would do well, if you are guilty, to confess and give glory to God." She replied: "I am as clear as the child unborn."

Judge Hathorne exclaimed: "Is it not an unaccountable case, that when you are examined these persons are afflicted?"

She said: "I have nobody to look to but God."

Dorcas Good—a child not five years of age—was arrested and tried by this kind of testimony on a charge of being a witch; accused of biting, pinching, and choking the afflicted children. She was sent to prison, but was not hanged.

In those days many of influence and position suffered. Thus Philip English—a merchant prince—was arrested, together with his wife, who was a lady of refinement and culture; they were accused of witchcraft, and were sent to jail in Boston; but by the assistance of two clergymen of that city they escaped, and went to New York, where they remained until the excitement subsided, when they returned to their home.

Mrs. Susannah Martin was charged with witchcraft, because her clothes were clean. On being asked how it was that her clothes were dry, she exclaimed, "I scorn to have a drabbled dress." She was, of course, sent to prison.

When one George Jacobs was tried, the Judge said: "Look, then, she accuseth you to your face; she chargeth you that you hurt her twice."

Jacobs replied: "It is not true; what would you have me say? I never wronged no man, in word nor deed."

Says the Judge: "Here are three evidences."

Jacobs replies: "You tax me for a wizard; you may as well tax me for a buzzard. I have done no harm." The Judge replies: "Is it no harm to afflict these?"

The Judges here accept the spectre doctrine—endorse the prevailing belief—that the seeing or professed seeing of a spectre of a person accused, in the form of a bird or beast, by the afflicted children (the accusers), was proof of the person accused being in league with the devil.

Says the Judge: "How comes it to be your appearance?"

Jacobs answers: "The devil can take any likeness."

Observe, here, the prisoner himself admits the delusion under which he was to be murdered.

Rebecca Jacobs, wife of George Jacobs, Jr., had

been for years known to be insane; her daughter, as well as her father-in-law, had been imprisoned; her husband had been exiled; and at last she was arrested, taken away from her children—those of them who were old enough to walk following her, crying piteously—and sent to jail.

When Mrs. How was called up for trial the Judge says: "What say you to this charge? here are them which charge you with witchcraft."

"If it was the last moment I was to live, God knows I am innocent of anything in this nature," she replies.

We are told that "the girls were continually knocked down by a glance of her eye, and brought out of a fit by touching her. When they attempted to approach her, they were prostrated as if by a violent shock of electricity."

The Judge asks Mrs. How, "What do you say to these things? they cannot come to you."

She replied: "Sir, I am not able to give account of it."

"Cannot you tell what keeps them off from your body?" says the Judge.

She replies: "I cannot tell, I know not what it is."

"That is strange," said the Judge, "that you should do these things, and not be able to tell how."

Here, as usual, the Judge assumes the genuineness of the spectre evidence—the testimony of these entranced, hysterical, insane girls. Mrs. How, with many other accused persons, was led in chains to jail.

The following conversation in court, between Judge Hathorne and one of the accused—Bridget Bishop—is interesting. The court says:

"They say you bewitched your first husband to death."

"If it please your worship, I know nothing of it."

Mrs. Bishop shakes her head, and the afflicted shake their heads at the same time; when she nods her head, they are tortured.

Judge Hathorne says: "How is it that your appearance doth hurt these?"

She says: "I am innocent."

Judge Hathorne says: "Why, you seem to act witchcraft before us by the motions of your body, which seem to have influence upon the afflicted."

She replies: "I am innocent, I know not what a witch is."

The Judge asks: "How do you know, then, that you are not a witch?"

She answers: "I do not know what you say."

The Judge says: "How can you know that you are not a witch, and yet not know what a witch is?"

She replies: "I am clear; if I were such a person, you should know it."

In none of these trials do the accused have any counsel;—the judges; the afflicted children, who were the accusers; the prisoners, who were accused by the children; the jury; the people, who came in crowds from long distances, and sometimes interrupted the proceedings with voluntary, extemporaneous testimony against the prisoners, constituted the court.

It is said that there was no hope of escape for those who were tried, as by the dogma of the trustworthiness of spectre testimony there could not be; trial meant conviction; conviction meant death. "The path from the jail, *through the court*, led only to Gallows Hill."

When Mrs. Nurse was tried, and—on account of a difficulty of hearing and the confusion amid the abuse—failed to make a satisfactory explanation, was convicted, after having been once acquitted, an attempt was made to influence Governor Phipps to save her from the gallows, but without success; and, after being excommunicated from her church, she was hanged on Witches' Hill.

It is asserted, though not absolutely proved, that during those trials a vigilance committee existed in the town, the duties of which were to co-operate with the magistrates to bring the accused to trial, and to see that they obtained what was called justice. It is believed that the influence of this committee kept the Governor from interfering to save the victims from the gallows.

It is creditable to our times that, during the hottest part of the Guiteau excitement, vigilance committees

—though often talked of—were never fairly organized. Mason and Jones, who shot at Guiteau, were without any accomplices in their attempts at murder; although the American people regretted at the time that they failed.

Unusual strength of body and mind was always regarded as evidence of being possessed of the devil, and in Salem evidence of this kind supplemented the spectral evidence.

A clergyman named Burroughs, who had been unpopular in Salem, and had removed to another place, was charged with being unusually strong. It was stated "that he carried a barrel of cider from a canoe to the shore; that he could travel as fast as a horse; and that he held out a gun, with seven feet barrel, with only putting the forefinger of his right hand into the muzzle." This was testimony sufficient, and more than sufficient, to convict him; and he was speedily and conscientiously convicted and sentenced to be hanged.

George Jacobs, Senior, eighty-one years of age, supported by crutches, when told that the girls had accused him of being in league with the devil to afflict them, replied: "Let them prove it, and I stand under it." He appealed to God, and to the record of a thirty-three years' residence in Salem. He was tried, convicted, and killed; his son, charged with the same crime, fled to a foreign shore; and his son's insane wife was sent to prison on the same charge.

It is probable, or at least quite possible, that other victims either were insane or became so through their afflictions.

The Rev. Mr. Lawson, in the early part of the excitement, preached a sermon that was very popular at the time, in which he said: "And whosoever hath observed these things must needs be convinced that the motions of the persons afflicted, both as to the manner and as to the violence of them, are the mere effects of diabolical malice and operations, and that it cannot rationally be imagined to proceed from any other source."

He further says: "He (Satan) contracts and indents with witches and wizards, that they shall be the instruments by whom he may more affect and afflict the bodies and minds of others." He calls upon Christians, saying: "Arm, arm, arm! and let us admit no parley, give no quarter; let none of Satan's forces or furies be more vigilant to hurt us than we are to resist and oppress them." He calls upon the magistrates to "check and rebuke Satan." This sermon of Mr. Lawson was at once printed, indorsed by the Boston ministers, and dedicated to the presiding magistrates and the pastors of the Mother Church at Salem. The Guiteau trial called forth thousands of sermons of a similar character.

The outside mob influenced the trial, indirectly and directly, by outcries, by interruptions in court, and by threatening the judges and prosecutors, if they did not do their duty; and in one case the judges yielded, and when the jury brought in a verdict of not guilty, they were sent out again, to return with a verdict of guilty.

The active, controlling leaders in the Salem trials were the leaders of the three great professions—theology, medicine, and law—who were more violent than the people in their charges against the accused, and in the urgency and vehemence of their desire to have them destroyed.

TESTIMONY OF CONFESSIONS.

Spectral testimony was reinforced by the confessions of many of the accused; indeed, of the persons who were accused many escaped hanging by confessing; some of these admitted that they were in league with the devil; that they had signed the devil's book; that they had been baptized by his majesty, and had attended mock sacraments. These confessions were given frequently, with large detail in places, dates, and circumstances. Mrs. Osgood, for example, confessed that the devil appeared to her in the shape of a cat; others spoke of trips through the air on sticks, and of inflicting tortures on their accusers; even children confessed against their parents. These confessions were mostly insincere, and were wrung, and pressed out of the victims in order that they might save their lives; sometimes under torture, sometimes under the entreaties of friends, and in some cases, not unlikely in all sincerity, through the delusions of trance or insanity, some may have really seen, or thought they saw, the spectres, and really believed themselves in confederacy with the spirit of evil. These confessions were regarded as confirmatory evidence of spectral testimony, and those who doubted were brought face to face with these confessions and asked if they did not convince them of the solidity and truth of witchcraft; and there was no answer.

SALEM WITCHCRAFT TRIALS COMPARED WITH THE TRIALS OF CADET WHITTAKER AND GUITEAU.

In the Salem witchcraft trials, the phenomena of insanity, hysteria, and trance appeared both in the accusers—the afflicted children—and, to a certain extent, in some of the accused.

In the Guiteau trial the phenomena of insanity were exhibited by the prisoner in court to a degree without precedent in the history of jurisprudence; but the prosecutors were perfectly sane, and also perfectly non-expert on the subject of insanity.

The parallelism between the two excitements—that in Salem and that in regard to Guiteau—is as follows:

First, both trials were the result of ignorance of the nervous system in disease—that of Guiteau, ignorance of insanity; the Salem trials, ignorance of insanity, hysteria, trance, and allied states, more complex phenomena than those of insanity alone, but all referable to the nervous system.

Had these nervous phenomena been understood, there would have been no trials of witches in Salem, and no trial of Guiteau in Washington.

Secondly, the trials in Salem, like the trial in Washington, were the result of a worn-out English dogma at once unscientific and merciless, which was destined to be rejected after the trials were over.

In the Salem trials Chief-Justice Stoughton rendered, and all through adhered to, the decision, that spectral testimony, the seeing of apparitions by the afflicted children, was admissible, and must be received; and when, therefore, these children swore they saw, or professed to see, the apparitions of the prisoners in the form of birds or animals engaged in diabolical work, they were obliged to bring in a verdict of guilty, and so they did in every case. Such a verdict was a logically inevitable result of the decision of the Chief-Justice.

On the Guiteau trial Judge Cox decided that a knowledge of right and wrong was evidence of responsibility; and as Guiteau, like nearly all other insane murderers, knew right from wrong, and as with the insane generally, murdered because murder was a dreadful thing to do, there was for the jury no choice; they must bring in a verdict of guilty.

In Salem the very proofs, symptoms, certain signs of insanity, hysteria, and trance were interpreted as certain signs and proofs of witchcraft; the worse the afflicted children behaved, the more weight was given to their testimony; accumulation of evidence which to an expert in the nervous system, had there been any at that time, would have been known to establish the innocence of the accused, was, by the rules of evidence, regarded as accumulation of evidence of their guilt.

In the Guiteau trial, the more insanity was poured forth, the more abundant the proofs of an insane life that were arrayed, the more thoroughly were the court and country convinced of the sanity of the prisoner—had there been less evidence of insanity in his case, he might have been acquitted.

A proof that the dogma that knowledge of right and wrong is a test of responsibility—under which Guiteau was convicted, and which, if carried out, would convict about every lunatic murderer ever driven before a court—is dying out in England, where it originated, and will die in America. Even as I write these lines, Maclean, who, probably incited by the trial of Guiteau, fired a pistol at the Queen, was acquitted on the plea of insanity, after five minutes' deliberation by the jury, although there was not brought into court one thousandth part as much evidence of insanity as in the case of Guiteau; and although he knew what he was doing when he shot at the Queen quite as well as Guiteau when he shot President Garfield.

The dogma that a knowledge of right and wrong is a proof of responsibility still exists in English law-books; but practically it is disregarded in important cases.

There is no civilized country except America that would have even tried Guiteau, to say nothing of convicting him. The parallelism here between the Salem trials and the Guiteau trial is direct and complete. Although the dogma by which the Salem murders were carried out was of English birth, yet the trials of that day would have been impossible in England, or in any other country than America; just as the Guiteau trial would been impossible in any other country than America. Yet, further, after the Salem excitement began to subside, then the propriety of admitting spectre evidence began to be more and more doubted, until it was entirely rejected; so, now, ever since the trial of Guiteau—especially since the publication of the views of the leading experts in diseases of the nervous system, some of whom did not testify in court—the opinion that his trial and conviction were disgraceful has been gaining ground throughout the country.

To the eyes of modern psychology this spectre evidence on which our fathers and mothers in Salem were convicted was—so far as it goes—a proof of the innocence of the victims; for we know it to be purely subjective, coming from the brain of the accusers, and having no objective existence.

The parallelism between the Salem witchcraft trials and the trial of Cadet Whittaker at West Point and New York is in this: That in both cases spectral evidence was admitted, and by spectral evidence alone, or mainly, the accused were convicted.

The spectral evidence in the Salem trials was that the accusers saw yellow-birds, or cats, or hogs, or black dogs, that were supposed to represent the apparitions of the accused persons in voluntary league with the devil.

The spectral evidence, on the trial of Cadet Whittaker, was that the experts in handwriting, hired by the accusers, saw, or thought they saw, or swore that they thought they saw, minute resemblances between the handwriting of Cadet Whittaker and the note of warning found in his room. This testimony, if sincere, was subjective, coming from the brains of the experts, and having no demonstrable objective existence; as was established on the trial by those who are authorities on the nervous system and in the use of the microscope. The handwriting experts for the prosecution on the Cadet Whittaker trials saw, or declared that they saw, whatever they were looking for; whatever they were hired to see; whatever they thought was necessary to see, in order to secure the conviction of the accused; precisely so in Salem.*

Cadet Whittaker, when found by the officers of the Post at West Point, was in a state of genuine unconsciousness from fright, having been, to use college language, "hazed" during the night, according to a frequent custom in American institutions of learning; although his physical injuries were very trifling indeed, he was scared into unconsciousness, as is not unfrequently the case with timid natures.

In this there was nothing remarkable or terrible, the physical injuries being insignificant and the recovery from mental disturbance only a matter of a few hours; but Whittaker was at once accused of having mutilated himself and of feigning unconsciousness, and this accusation gave rise to a Court of Inquiry at West Point and a subsequent court-martial of many months duration in New York, asked for by the accused and granted by President Hayes.

* One illustration of spectral testimony is the following: Abigail Williams calls out the name of one of the accused and says: "Look where she sits upon the beam, sucking her yellow-bird, betwixt her fingers." Ann Putnam chimed in, "There is a yellow-bird sitting on the minister's hat, as it hangs on the pin in the pulpit." This spectral testimony was illustrated by trance subjects in my lecture before the New York Academy of Science.

These trials of Cadet Whittaker have no exact precedent in the history of mankind; the nearest parallels in this country being the Salem witchcraft trials, and here the parallelism being mainly in the admission of spectral evidence.

One proof that the handwriting testimony, by which Whittaker was mainly convicted, on both the trials, was subjective and spectral rather than objective and scientific, was the fact that there was no agreement among the experts until they knew what to look for; they saw what they were expected to see, or what it was desired they should see; in comparing the note of warning with specimens of the handwriting of the cadets, the names not being known, there was no agreement; for they knew not what they were to look for; but when handwriting which they knew to be Whittaker's was compared with the note of warning, they at once saw resemblances, as they were expected to do; but the resemblances were in the brains of the experts; as the cats, dogs, and yellow-birds of Salem were in the brains of the afflicted children.

When Ex-Governor Chamberlain—the counsel for Cadet Whittaker on the subsequent court-martial—asked me to examine the medical side of the case, and to explain the nervous phenomena exhibited by Whittaker, I said to him that there was really no need of expert testimony on the medical side;

that there was no evidence whatever against Whittaker, and none that could be brought; that even if he were guilty he could not be proved guilty, and that the only advantage of the testimony that I gave was that it would be a positive and scientific explanation of the mystery of the case.

This opinion has since been practically confirmed by all the authorities in Washington who have reviewed the case, including the Judge-Advocate-General, Secretary Lincoln, the Attorney-General, and President Arthur.

COMPARISON OF THE MISTAKES IN DIAGNOSIS OF PHYSICIANS IN SALEM AND IN WASHINGTON.

In the case of Guiteau, the physicians and politicians who were first called in to make a diagnosis mistook the symptoms of insanity for the symptoms of wickedness; an error which is quite as natural for non-experts in insanity in our time as that of the village physician of Salem, Dr. Griggs, in witchcraft times, in attributing the phenomena of trance and insanity to possession of the devil. If the physicians in and near Salem had known something of the nervous system, and been bold enough to declare their knowledge, there would have been no executions and no trials; for there would have been nothing to try. If the politicians and physicians who were summoned to study the case of Guiteau had known enough of that form of insanity that he so strikingly represents to have made a diagnosis of the case, there would have been no lengthy trial and no conviction; for a lunatic can commit no crime. There is only one way in which a lunatic can be legally punished; that is by swearing that he is not a lunatic, as was done in Washington; by adhering to and insisting on the dogma that if a man knows right from wrong he is not—in a legal sense—insane. By this dogma lunatics who commit murders could very rarely escape; since nearly every crazy man who has force enough to murder not only knows right from wrong. but he murders simply because murdering is a terrible thing to do. In Washington it was well understood that a lunatic could commit no crime; indeed, it was about the only thing connected with insanity that was understood by the court or by the lawyers on either side; hence the orders went forth and were properly executed that those who were to testify should say that insanity was not insanity, that insanity was not hereditary, and that the prisoner was sane, and consequently entirely responsible.

This line of testimony—to deny under oath facts of science which were as well established as the Copernican theory—was settled and determined on by physicians and politicians in caucus assembled, and was adhered to persistently and consistently by a number of those who gave testimony. They did more; they parceled out their non-expertness and perjury among them, as so many pieces of silver, assigning to one the denial of this scientific truth, to another the denial of that, until, out of all, a spherical mass of delusion could be evolved that should make it plausible as well as popular to hang the crazy.

The brother of Guiteau testified in my presence, in Washington, that he believed that his brother—the assassin—was possessed of the devil; that he had voluntarily given himself over to the devil, to serve his vile purposes; he also testified that his father had brought him up in this witchcraft belief, and that he had always explained his brother's conduct by this theory of possession, which was precisely the belief which in Salem gave rise to the excitement of 1692.

The brother further testified that—under the influence of this theory—he at one time seized the assassin and turned him out of his office, not only in an unbrotherly but in an unkind, rough, and cruel manner, for which he now publicly apologized. He further testified that he had abandoned this witchcraft theory in regard to his brother since the assassination; but he did not state that he had abandoned the general belief in witchcraft. From this testimony —to every word of which I listened with interest as well as with astonishment, since nothing like it has probably been heard in court from the lips of a white man during the past one hundred years—it is probable that the Guiteau family, part of them at least, are survivors of the Salem and the seventeenth century superstition; and it is also clear that but for this survival of witchcraft belief in that family, President Garfield would now be alive; for the error in diagnosis, mistaking the symptoms of insanity for possession by the devil, would not have been made by the relatives and friends of Guiteau, and the future assassin would have been placed under guardianship, either in or out of an asylum.

ATTACKS OF DESPOTISM.

Before and during the Guiteau trial the press of this country suffered from one of those attacks of despotism which are the price that we are obliged at times to pay for our general liberty; instead of one Czar we had fifty million Czars, so that out of about eight thousand papers there were—for a time—but one or two that dared to speak for the truth. Until speaking for the truth could do little or no good no press, no pulpit was strong enough to take the right side; but all through in this, as in all popular excitements, the press and the pulpit were like ships on the bosom of the sea, rising and falling with the tide. In Prussia and in Russia there was more freedom of the press for a few months than in America, on this special topic of Guiteau. An editor whose sympathies were with science and truth told me that he dared not say so, except in private; and a very prominent journal that sent for my views was frightened on learning that they were on the right side, and—as I predicted—could not then publish them, though it did so subsequently and repeatedly. This attack of despotism—like similar attacks on other themes that periodically afflict our country—ran its course, like a fever; and very soon these same journals found it not only safe but expedient to give science a hearing. Had there been many newspapers in Salem days their voice would have been unanimous that society must be protected.

The record of the term of the court which opened in Salem the first week in June cannot be found. It is supposed that it was destroyed by those who wished that the details of those bloody and cruel deeds should perish from the memory of man. It is probable that the children of those who took an active part in those massacres preferred the crime of stealing the records to the shame of having them read by posterity. The time will soon come, if indeed it have not come already, when all those who directly took part in the prosecution of Guiteau will blush or turn pale at the mention of his name, and will wish that the records of those savage scenes in

Washington in which they were participants could also be erased from the memories of men.

Near the close of the Guiteau trial, an eminent student of the nervous system in Germany wrote me, asking me to send him the records of the trial, if I could obtain them. In reply, I was obliged to say that I would be glad to accommodate him, but that the record of the trial was valueless to science and a dishonor to our nation.

An accompaniment of the Salem trials was the excommunication from the church of those who were condemned for witchcraft, whether sane or insane. Martha Corey, who "concluded her life by an eminent prayer upon the ladder," was excommunicated the day after she was sentenced to death.

Guiteau was also excommunicated from the church, not as a result of the trial, or of the murder of the President, but for other insane acts committed by him years before; but during and after the trial he was deprived almost entirely not only of Christian consolation, but of all attempts to reform or influence him, even by those who were under the delusion that he was sane. In this respect the insane of witchcraft days were treated more kindly than Guiteau, for they were visited, prayed with, and prayed for, by the clergy, by the people, and by friends, sometimes for long periods before they were arraigned in court. The most popular Presbyterian clergyman in the country publicly stated in his pulpit, as was reported, that he felt that he could not pray for Guiteau: and in that feeling he represented very fairly the Christian church and the American people.

It would be an investigation of interest and one which a psychologist might undertake, to find out how many of the insane of our country—both in and out of asylums—have been excommunicated from the church, as a punishment for their insane acts, as was Guiteau and as were the victims of the Salem witchcraft excitement.

SPEEDY JUSTICE IN SALEM.

All these things—the commitments, trials, and executions—were accomplished in the course of a few days, or, at most, weeks; had there been delays of law, as we have now, probably there would have been very few, if any, executions.

The first warrants for arrest were issued on the 29th of February, 1692. On April 4th, of the same year, a council was held at Salem to try the witches.

On the 4th of May, of the same year, Sir Wm. Phipps, the Governor, arrived at Boston from England. A special court was now appointed by the Governor to try these witchcraft cases. It is now held that this court was illegally appointed, and that it required the concurrence of the House of

Representatives. If they had waited for the House of Representatives to assemble, the excitement would have been over, and there would probably have been no more executions; another argument for the delays of law. This court re-assembled June 29th, of the same year, having meantime had an adjournment or intermission, during which the clergy and others were consulted. The court was to have re-assembled the first Tuesday of November, but it never met again. In June one person was hanged; in July, five; in August, five; in September, eight, including the pressing to death of Giles Corey.

In our time, with the present checks and delays of law, which cause so much annoyance to the press and the people, none of these convicted persons would have been hanged; they would all probably have been liberated, as were hundreds of others who were arrested and convicted.

MURDERS STOPPED BY THE ACCUSERS STRIKING TOO HIGH.

The wife of Governor Phipps had been accused; the Rev. Samuel Willard also was charged with witchcraft; but the presiding Judge told the girl that she had made a mistake, and ordered her removal from the room. Rev. Mr. Hale, of Beverly, had been active in the prosecutions; but when his own wife—

a lady of eminent piety and great usefulness—was struck at, he began to see that he had been deluded.* When the judges stopped condemning, the people stopped accusing.

HOW AFFLICTED CHILDREN ARE TREATED IN THESE DAYS.

If the afflicted children had been treated at that time as we treat similar cases now, there would have been no trials and no murders. When children act as these afflicted children acted, become hysterical and entranced through emotional excitement, we have, to-day, simple and effective remedies—*separation, sedatives,* and, in some cases, *discipline.* My studies of the nervous system have many times led me into circles quite as superstitious and grotesque as the circle that constituted the accusers in the witchcraft trials. At the Home of the Eddy Brothers, in Vermont, whither were drawn by psychical attraction the most superstitions of the most superstitious of this whole nation, I saw a typical and perfect survival of Salem days and Salem character.

---

* When Mr. Hobbs—a man of wealth and friends—was accused, his bond of one thousand dollars was paid by his friends, to save him from appearing in court, and thus his life was saved ; and when the storm had passed he returned to his home.

Capt. John Alden, of the Provincial Navy, escaped from jail, was secreted by friends in Duxbury, and was saved.

It was as though our fathers of the seventeenth century had arisen in all their simplicity, non-expertness, and conscientiousness; it was the past surviving in the present; and as history is best studied through the present, there could have been no better chance to study the psychology of witchcraft, in which most of them were believers; and this opportunity, as best I could, I improved. I joined circles the members of which developed the phenomena both of trance and hysteria, and some of whom were already nearly, if not quite insane, and really saw and heard whatever they expected or wished to see and hear—forms of loved ones who had passed away—a resurrection of those who had been buried for centuries.

These phenomena were accompanied in some cases by spasms, cries, and tears, such as the afflicted children of Salem exhibited when brought near those whom they accused of bewitching them.

NO SPECIAL LAW FOR SALEM TRIALS.

Most noteworthy is this fact, that the witchcraft trials in Salem were carried out under no special colonial law enacted with reference to the subject, but under an old law enacted by James I. of England; but after the excitement was all over, a special law was enacted in the province, based on the old English law.

This law was enacted by the judges and the friends of the judges, who were responsible for the Salem murders; another proof that many phases of delusion linger longer in law than in any other profession, and that legislation and jurisprudence are always far behind and out of sight both of science and of truth.

It cannot be repeated too often, nor under too many forms, that the clergymen of New England were the first of professional leaders to oppose the excitement and the cruelty; the first to see the errors and to endeavor to disabuse the people; and it is the clergymen more than any other class that have been blamed for what happened. The conduct of the doctors was—as we have seen—unanimously non-expert.

At a session of the Superior Court, held in Salem in 1693, Lieutenant-Governor Stoughton, who had presided at the witchcraft trials, was Chief-Justice. Spectre evidence was ruled out, the court saying, when asked how much it was worth, "As much as of chips in wort."

The dogma, therefore, under which the convictions had been obtained was now abandoned; and in subsequent sessions the trials resulted in acquittals. The Governor now opened the prison doors to those suspected and accused; hundreds were set free; never before or since was there such a jail delivery in New England.

Two years after the excitement of 1692 the General Court reversed the attainders of persons who had suffered under the witchcraft delusion, and gave money compensation to their families; but in doing so, stated that evil spirits caused the trials and convictions; thus showing that they were no less superstitious in their acts of justice than they had been in their acts of injustice.

At this very hour, in and around Salem and adjacent Massachusetts towns, witchcraft is cherished by the sons and daughters of these Puritans; they may not know or confess that they are believers in the delusion, and the fact of such belief would only be brought out by close cross-examinations, which I have sometimes made; the belief is passive rather than active; .they would shed the blood of no one, not even their own; but in this doctrine, the root, the basis, the life, the soul of witchcraft—that the devil enters into and takes possession of men, and binds them over to himself—they have, some of them, made no advance, or but little advance, over their Puritan ancestors of 1692.

TURNING OF THE TIDE.

It was three years before the tide fully turned; not until 1695 was it thoroughly safe to speak for truth, justice, and mercy on this matter in Salem.

In 1882 the tide of popular feeling began to turn

much sooner. In less than two months from the conclusion of the Guiteau trial it became almost, and in less than four months it became quite safe, in moderately intelligent circles, to speak for science against delusion, and to publicly as well as privately declare that since the witchcraft trials and executions of Salem no blacker picture has appeared in our national history than that exhibited in the court-room in Washington.

On the 20th of July, 1702—ten years after the Salem slaughter—a bill was ordered by the House of Representatives, referring to the trials for witchcraft of 1692, declaring that spectre evidence should not thereafter be used to take away the life or good name of persons within the Province; and that those who had been convicted by such evidence should be—as far as possible—restored in credit, reputation, and estate.

PSYCHOLOGY OF DELUSIONS—GENUINE PHENOMENA *vs.* IMPOSTURE.

Why do we believe in witchcraft, in astrology, in alchemy, in spiritualism, and why have these beliefs been stronger forces in society than all the sciences of all the ages? These questions science can now answer.

The universe, in its relation to the very weak and limited organ, the human brain, has these three general divisions—the demonstrably true, or science; the demonstrably false, or delusions; and the indemonstrable; under the last division comes religion. What we call truth and error, are relative, not absolute, relative to and changing with the age, the environment, the race, the person, the moods of the hour, of the moment, that which is true to one being false to another, and false to the one at another time of life, and to others perhaps indemonstrable. These three territories are elastic and mobile, like clouds, and have fluctuating and shifting boundaries; phenomena which at one time are referred to religion, at another time are referred to delusion, later still to science; superstition or delusion being religion out of fashion, and science the organized knowledge of nature. Of these three divisions science, being related to the reason, is infinitesimally small, while the indemonstrably and demonstrably false, being related to the emotions, the chief elements in the human mind, are infinitely large. Science can make no advance except at the expense of delusions or of the indemonstrable; wise, therefore, are the instincts of delusionists in their hereditary dread and dislike of science, for it is their one and only enemy; the instinct of self-preservation being as strong in delusions as in realities.

Under the second and third of these divisions, the demonstrably false and indemonstrable, formerly came witchcraft. Now that these phenomena, are proved to be false, it comes exclusively under the second head—delusions—and some of its phenomena can be claimed for science.

The weaker and more immature the mind, the farther it extends its imaginings, and the less it heeds what is immediately above us; the child studies the stars before it studies its own eyes by which it sees the stars. In the active stages of certain forms of hopeless and helpless insanity, the patient has delusions of measureless greatness; the ragged beggar is a millionaire, scattering millions; the tramp an emperor, or the emperor's emperor, the king of kings. This law of the correlation of feebleness of mental force with immensity of imaginings is universal; the less we know the more we dream; such is the psychology of reverie or building castles in the air; such is the psychology of witchcraft. For the undeveloped mind, nature is too mean or small a thing; only in the supernatural—the infinite above and outside of nature—can there be found proper food for emotions that are ever hungry for what cannot be proved. As a minute object held close to a lamp casts a long shadow on a distant wall, so a little thought projected into infinity, becomes infinite in extent. Such a shadow was witchcraft, which for centuries darkened our rising civilization. (For further analysis and definitions of superstition, delusion, and so forth, see Appendix A).

That there was more or less of imposture commingled with the trance, hysteria and insanity which were at the basis of the Salem excitement; that the genuine symptoms of real disease were supplemented by malignity and crime; that, in short, unintentional deception was reinforced by intentional deception, both on the part of the "afflicted children" and of those who co-operated with them in and out of court, is more than probable, reasoning deductively, from the established principles of human nature and the known facts of history, and from what we see about us day by day.

Superstition is the mother of imposture; when any untruth is strongly and firmly believed it begets a large family of frauds which would never have been born or even conceived, but for the delusion of which they are the offspring.

Thus alchemy—the belief that the baser metals can be changed into gold—produced an army of frauds and impostors who made cheating a business, and became experts in the art of professing to do that which no human being can do, and which they themselves knew was impossible to themselves, however possible it might be to others; thus astrology—a belief in the directing and controlling influence of the stars over human character and events—made it easy for astrologers to make a living without telling the truth, non-experts in astronomy attaining the highest expertness in lying; thus at this enlightened hour the fading belief in spiritualism—the dogma that the spirits of the departed communicate to the senses of the living facts and fancies from another world—which belief is, to our time and to this later civilization what astrology, alchemy and witchcraft were to the earlier civilization—has developed a new profession in modern society, that of mediums; who, while half believing in the delusion are supported mainly by those who believe nothing else.

In psychology, if not in theology, the doctrine of the trinity is verifiable; in a single person we shall find the deceiver, the partially deceived and the wholly deceived; three in one and one in three; unity in diversity and diversity in unity; sundry and distinct colors uniting pattern; three streams flowing together in one, yet with three currents; an engrafted tree bearing varied fruits, all nourished from a common trunk, and rooted in the soil of superstition.

When we do anything under excitement we are rarely able to analyze—indeed rarely attempt to analyze—our motives for what we do; whether they are or are not sincere is a question that mobs of any name would find it hard to answer.

Even in what is undertaken quietly—in that which becomes a life-habit of labor—the connection between motive and result is beyond the tracing of most minds, however analytical or introspective. The stream of conduct flows from many sources; and to determine mathematically which supplies the largest volume of motives surpasses the computative power of the human intellect; we are often deceived when we suppose we are deceivers; dupes even more than charlatans; cheating ourselves more successfully than we are cheating others; mingling the false with the true so well that neither we nor others shall distinguish; and as in crossing the Atlantic we soon lose sight of the shores whence we sail, so in a long course of conduct, the inspiring motive to that conduct passes from sight and even from memory.

The hysterical and entranced children who were the chief accusers in the Salem witchcraft trials could not probably themselves have told just how far they were or were not sincere;* the keenest psychologist could not have marked out the dividing line between the symptoms of trance and hysteria and the symptoms of imposture; lying is one of the symptoms of hysteria.

I often see, professionally, hysterical men and hysterical women deceive themselves and others without knowing that they are deceiving, but who—like Carlyle—have a foundation of real physical suffering, on which they build an immense superstructure of imaginary pains and woes; but to whom the superstructure is as real and as terrible as the foundation.

*Ann Putnam, in her confession, expresses sorrow, but does not suggest that there was any intentional trickery or fraud.

The jurors by whose verdict the nineteen persons had been murdered, also published a confession, but gave no intimation of fraud on the part of any one.

CHAPTER II.

PRACTICAL APPLICATIONS.

The Salem witchcraft trials — psychologically analyzed—suggest to the world these four practical lessons.

First. The need of a radical reconstruction of the principles of evidence in science, in logic, and in law.

This need of a reconstruction of the premises of our reasoning, especially as relating to the phenomena of living human beings, is as imperative in our time as was the organization of the inductive philosophy in the time of Lord Bacon. The details of such a reconstruction I have outlined elsewhere. (Popular Science Monthly, May, June and July, 1878.)

Logic is a machine, like a mill, what it turns out depends upon what is put in it; as stones, by no manner of grinding can become flour, so error, though it pass through all the syllogisms of the world, cannot be changed to truth. In all history we shall not find more thoroughly logical or consistent proceedings than the trials and murders in Salem.

THE CONVICTIONS LOGICALLY OBTAINED. 53

Even the severest critics of those times and those deeds—those who wrote in repentance and in tears—have never answered, and never could answer, the cogent and inevitable reasoning by which the judges of Salem condemned their innocent neighbors and friends to undeserved disgrace, to painful and shameful death and dishonored burial.

The legal mind is usually a logical mind; and for this, partly if not mainly, the lawyers and jurists of that time were the last to give up their belief in the delusion; behind all others in their repentance. Even Judge Sewall, in his annual confession in public before the congregation, gave no reason for his confession, and could have given none, for there was none to give; by the principles of evidence inherited from non-expert English courts, by the precedents of judges upon judges (ignorant of psychology as they were learned in law), the convictions and executions at Salem were legitimate, necessary, and biblical; it would have been a crime if the accused had not been convicted. Nor was there any logical reason why the colony was not extirpated. The reasoning by which the first victim was hanged was sufficient to convict and hang every human being on the surface of the globe. It was not by any course of reasoning; it was not by any process of logic; it was in spite of and against all logic, and in the teeth of the principles of evidence which the lawyers were a unit in accepting, that the judicial murders were arrested.

THE TWO DOGMAS.

There is and was more evidence in favor of the truth of witchcraft, millions to one, than in favor of the Copernican theory, or of any other established fact of science. The advantage the Copernican theory has over witchcraft, is that it is sustained by experts. To compare the bulk and mass of evidence of witchcraft with the bulk and mass of evidence in favor of the Copernican theory, is like weighing the earth against a pebble.

On this subject Mr. Lecky adds: "And yet it is, I think, difficult to examine the subject with impartiality without coming to the conclusion that the historical evidence establishing the reality of witchcraft is so vast and so varied that it is impossible to disbelieve it without what—on other subjects—we should deem the most extraordinary rashness. The defenders of the belief—who were often men of great and distinguished talent—maintained that there was no fact in all history more fully attested, and that to reject it would be to strike at the root of all historical evidence of the miraculous. The belief implied the continual recurrence of facts of the most extraordinary and impressive character, and of such a nature as to fall strictly within human cognizance."

"The subject, as we have seen, was examined in tens of thousands of cases, in almost every country of Europe, by tribunals which included the acutest lawyers and ecclesiastics of the age, on the scene, and at the time when the alleged acts had taken place, and with the assistance of innumerable witnesses."

"The judges had no motives whatever for desiring the condemnation of the accused; and as conviction would be followed by a fearful death, they had, on the contrary, the strongest motives to exercise their power with caution and deliberation.

The whole force of public opinion was directed constantly and earnestly to the question for many centuries; and although there was some controversy concerning the details of witchcraft, the fact of its existence was long considered undoubted."

Giles Corey, when urged by his friend to confess, in hope of saving his life, replied, in Longfellow's language:

> "I will not plead.
> If I deny, I am condemned already
> In courts where ghosts appear as witnesses,
> And swear men's lives away."

In the Salem witchcraft trials, not a few confessed themselves guilty of that of which they were innocent; some no doubt really believed they were guilty of that with which they were charged; others confessed, it may be, to escape imprisonment.

PRACTICAL APPLICATIONS.

The people in and around Salem, after the trials were over, and the excitement had passed away, retained as firmly as ever their belief in the delusion of witchcraft; and in their disappointment they declared that the kingdom of Satan had prevailed, and that they were a God-forsaken people for their leniency to witches.

One of the most interesting facts connected with these cases was that the accused—many of them at least—were such firm believers in the doctrines of witchcraft that they yielded to their fate without complaint; they knew and felt that they had condemned others on the same testimony. They could not blame the judges, for they would have convicted any one else on the same evidence; they could not explain the mystery, and they felt, with Rev. Mr. Burroughs, that it was "an amazing providence," and they had only to submit to it, looking to God for strength and comfort.

The only difference of opinion, during the witchcraft excitement, among the leaders of the three professions, the clergymen, the physicians, the lawyers, and also the statesmen, was in regard to the question whether spectral evidence, the seeing or the professed seeing of the apparitions of the accused in the form of cats, dogs, hogs, birds, etc., was proof that the accused were in *voluntary* league with the devil to do evil ; that it was proof that they were doing the devil's work, was admitted by all parties in every direction; the point of dispute being only this—whether their apparitions were proof that they gave themselves up *voluntarily* to the service of the devil, or whether they were taken against their will; and this question was much discussed; but all the weight of opinion, especially of the judges, was in favor of explaining the spectral evidence as proof of voluntary service of the devil on the part of the accused; hence it must be accepted; hence it was accepted; hence the trials, convictions, and executions.

The jurors who had condemned their innocent neighbors and friends to death made a public confession of their non-expertness and cruelty, to which confession all their names were signed; but this very confession showed that they were almost as superstitious as the savages of Central Africa. They gave no reason for thinking that their decisions were wrong, but simply stated that they had erred through ignorance.

The truth was that they had done just their duty, and nothing more; it was impossible—under the decisions of the court—for them to bring in any other verdict than guilty; just as it was impossible for the jury on the Guiteau trial to bring in any other verdict than guilty, on the theory that those who know right from wrong must be hanged if they commit murder.

Ann Putnam—who was one of those who had testified against the victims, and had been the means of bringing them to death, being at that time a child twelve years of age—made in 1706 a confession which was received at communion, twelve years after the massacre, in which she used this language:

"I desire to be humble before God for that sad and humbling providence that befel my father's family in the year about '92; that I, being then in my childhood, should, by such a providence of God, be made the instrument of accusing several persons of a grievous crime, whereby their lives were taken from them, who now, I have just ground and good reason to believe, they were innocent persons; and that it was a great delusion of Satan that deceived me in that sad time; whereby I justly fear I have been instrumental with others, though ignorantly and unwillingly, to bring upon myself and this land the guilt of innocent blood; though what was said or done by me against any person, I can truly and rightly say before God and man; I did it not out of anger, malice, or ill-will to any person, for I had no such thing against any one of them; but what I did was ignorantly, being deluded by Satan."

This lady was of a nervous organization, and was, no doubt, thrown into trances during the excitement. In her confession, as will be seen, she was as superstitious as in her accusation, for in both she laid the blame on the devil.

DELUSION FELL OF ITS OWN WEIGHT.

The Salem witchcraft delusion was broken, not by logic, nor truth, nor reason, nor religion, nor morality, nor even by charity; the arguments, the logic of the judges and the juries, were at no time successfully met, not even by the opposers of the delusion, during or after the excitement; indeed, the reasonings of the judges and the juries and the people were unanswerable then, and are unanswerable to-day, by any accepted principle of evidence. The murders were stopped, because the afflicted children aimed too high; they accused people of too great prominence like the Reverend Mr. Willard, a beloved clergyman of Boston, and they were ordered out of court. Their evidence against him was as logically strong as their evidence against the humblest citizens. In short, the Salem witchcraft excitement, like other similar excitements, fell of its own weight, unaffected then, and unaffected to-day, by any direct assaults of reason, truth, or science. The delusion to which the Guiteau trial gave public expression, that all insane people who know right from wrong should be punished for their misdeeds, is now being broken, not by logic nor by science, nor even by mercy, but only or mainly by the fact that men of wealth and power are charged with insanity. During the Guiteau trial other insane murderers have either not been tried or have been acquitted of murder (though they knew right from wrong, as the insane usually do) because they had influence, or because no one especially wished to kill them. Judges may go on deciding that a knowledge of right from wrong is a proof of responsibility, as the judges in Salem persisted, even after the violence had subsided, that spectral testimony was admissible in court, and must condemn the accused; but, just as in Salem, the influence of humanity and justice rose up and swept away the logic of courts and juries, and opened the prison doors to scores of condemned innocents; so, in our time, that most unjust and cruel dogma, that the knowledge of right and wrong is proof of responsibility, will never condemn any lunatic who has friends or money or public sympathy.

Even Mr. Upham, in his interesting *History of Witchcraft at Salem Village*, a work from which I derive many of these facts, and which I recommend to all who wish the details, uses this language:

"Sin, in all cases, when considered by a mind that surveys the whole field, is itself insanity." On the Guiteau trial some one said, or was reported to have said, that "moral insanity," whatever that may be, was "wickedness"; and fifty million people shouted approval. What the expression meant was not known, could not indeed be known to any human being; but the words sounded well; they were a call to battle and to blood, and the men and women of America breathed more freely as they heard them.

The Honorable Joseph Story, of the Supreme Court of the United States, in his Centennial address, says: "Our ancestors had no special reasons for shame in a belief which had the universal sanction of their own and all former ages; which counted in its train philosophers, as well as enthusiasts; which was graced by the learning of prelates, as well as by the countenance of kings; which the law supported by its mandates, and the purest judges felt no compunctions in enforcing. Let Witch Hill be for ever memorable by this sad catastrophe; not to perpetuate our dishonor, but as an affecting, enduring proof of human infirmity, a proof that perfect justice belongs to one judgment-seat only—that which is linked to the throne of God."

Make a few changes of words, and all this applies to our times, and to the trial of Guiteau. We have no special reasons for shame in trying this lunatic, since the belief that those who know right from wrong are always responsible, has the sanction of our own and the mother country. It has come down, a legacy of delusion, from generation to generation, and from court to court, tossed from one non-expert judge to another, until it has become as universally believed as it is untrue. The Judge could not do otherwise than accept this delusion, as the Judges in the Salem trials could not do otherwise than accept the delusion in the belief of spectral evidence; and the jury in the

Guiteau trial could not do otherwise than convict the insane person, as the jury in the Salem trials were obliged to convict their innocent neighbors and friends.

The horror of these trials in Salem and in Washington was not in the results of the trials, but in the processes—that there should have been any trial at all; the trial once begun, the issue was inevitable—conviction. In Salem, long after the force of the delusion had been broken, and peace had begun to succeed the gigantic storm, and a jail delivery had sent the survivors to their homes, yet even then, by the decision of the courts, trial led to conviction, trial was conviction, to be accused was to 'be hanged; the intervening processes, the arraignment and the pleading, the evidence for the prosecution and the defence, being but forms, having no power over the result. In Washington, Guiteau was convicted when he was arraigned; for, as some of the jurors have since said, the evidence on the trial had little or no influence with them.

In Chicago, I have seen, in one of the famous slaughter-houses of that city, the processes of killing and cleaning hogs: the animal is stabbed, cast on the platform and rolled over and over, and comes out with all his bristles removed, and as clean and white as a baby; unless snatched away, the result is as inevitable as gravity; and all come out alike, and clean alike. The courts in Salem and Washington were like these slaughter-houses; accepting the dogma of Salem, that spectral evidence must be received— accepting the theory at Washington, that those who know right from wrong must hang—then all those who are tried must come out at the gallows: the court being only the pathway to the scaffold, a piece of machinery by which living lunatics become dead lunatics. Our fathers were slain by a dogma; by a dogma Guiteau was convicted, and properly he should have been hanged before the trial, for the dogma—that those lunatics who know right from wrong should hang—makes a trial needless; such a dogma is the trial, and conviction and sentence all in one.

Secondly—Ignorance is the mother of cruelty. Our fathers and mothers in Salem were not despots, but non-experts; they would not have tried and murdered their brethren if they had known that they were innocent, any more than we would have tried and convicted Guiteau, if we had known that he was the most terribly insane man, of the type of insanity which he represents—religious monomania—ever before a court.

SUBJECTIVE MISTAKEN FOR OBJECTIVE PHENOMENA.

Confounding the subjective with the objective is the basis of half the delusions of the world. In the

Salem witchcraft trials there would have been no convictions, had not the subjective—that within the brain of the witness—been mistaken for the objective, that outside the brain. The human brain is as full of spectres as the sky is full of stars; and disease of the brain brings these spectres into view, as the darkness of night brings out the stars invisible by day. When we are awake and well, we do not see these spectres, for external nature occupies all our vision, as we do not see the stars by day, on account of the strong light of the sun; when we are sick in mind, or asleep, or even when we but close our eyes these spectres in infinite combination appear in view, like the myriads of stars in the firmament.

Even in science, men looking through a microscope see, too often, what they are looking for, confounding the subjective with the objective; that which they would like to see with what is to be seen. Experts in handwriting demonstrate this most interestingly; in the case of Cadet Whittaker, they saw whatever they were looking for; they could prove or disprove anything they wished.

PSYCHOLOGY THE YOUNGEST OF THE SCIENCES.

The study of disease has been discouraged because man cares least of all about himself, and what comes nearest to himself; in rising from savagery to barbarism, from barbarism to fractional civilization, and from fractional civilization to semi-civilization and the relative enlightenment of great nations, progress has been, not, as would be apparently most natural, from a knowledge of our own bodies in health and disease, and things that are nearest to us, towards things that are far away, but precisely the reverse. The young child when it looks out on nature does not ask what nature's laws are, but first of all, what is there above nature—a theologian from the moment it begins to think—and then it asks about the distant stars, the planets, the suns and their attendants; then, at a later age, about the earth, its form and size, the wild beasts that roam over it and the fishes that swim in the seas; then, at a still later date, it looks at the minute structure of inorganic nature—things that have no life; it becomes a physicist, a chemist and a botanist; and, later still, in but few cases, it asks about its own body, and how to care for it; last of all, and then in but one case out of thousands or millions, it asks about the mind, the highest fact in nature, and the fact concerning which one would think it would have begun its inquiries.

The newly-born babe, thrust suddenly on an unknown sea, thinks not and asks not from what port it sailed nor whence came its power to ask that or any other question, but to what port is it bound, and who rules the sea over which it is to sail.

I am studying now, and have been studying for some years, the mental growth of a little girl in my own family; and though I believe her prospects of developing psychological tastes are quite equal to those of other children of her age, I have never yet seen exhibited, or succeeded in developing in her very active, questioning mind, the faintest spark of interest in the problem of her own existence and growth. She points to the stars and asks—with Napoleon—"Who made all these?" But how *she* came to exist she does not inquire, nor for years will she be likely to inquire. Children vary, but this child is a type of humanity, and of the processes of development from barbarism toward civilization.

PSYCHOLOGY OF THE AMERICAN PEOPLE.

To answer the question why the last bloody battles of witchcraft were fought on American soil, it is needful to know something of the intellectual characteristics of the American people, and of the race to which they belong.

The Anglo-Saxon peoples in both Europe and America, have, in modern days, a genius for non-expertness in science. That we might preserve our political freedom we have in other directions become as slaves, bound in time-rusted chains of common delusions; we have sacrificed almost everything else that we might have liberty and stability. Were we not constantly nursed at the breast of Germany, both England and America would long since have starved to death scientifically, and even now this country is not yet emerged from its scientific marasmus. This genius for scientific non-expertness is attended by a genius of almost equal power for intellectual timidity. Of all great peoples the English speaking people are the most cowardly in the face of ideas; of such were our ancestors in England and New England; of such in fading degree are we at this hour. The one prayer of the puritan mother, that her child should never learn to think, has been answered, and thus far America has given no philosophy to the world. With all our opportunity, with all our advance, no other enlightened nation has expended so much cerebral force in the emotion of fear as America. Always our fathers were kept on the run before new truths; their ideals were lofty, they would be above the suspicion of science. Instinctively, as chickens run with cries from the shadow of a hawk flying high in the air, these puritans ran at the approach of new truths, hiding themselves in trembling terror under the broad wings of the church. Physical courage and moral courage our fathers possessed in abundant overflow, but in compensation they were wanting, as their sons are wanting now in intellectual courage; from this branch of their natures all the sap had been drawn, leaving it dwarfed, brittle, withered. More than half a century before an heroic band of cowards had landed on Plymouth Rock, and both they and their descendants were as timid in the presence of thought as they were brave against savages and persecution. The phrases "as timid as an Englishman," "as timid as an American" are likely to become current in the philosophic histories of the future.

Philistinism, so well described by Mr. Matthew Arnold and Mr. Richard Grant White, is, when analyzed psychologically, a combination of general intelligence, good nature, dullness and timidity. Any one of these qualities, or two of them, may exist in individuals of any race, but the combination of all four appears to belong to the modern Anglo-Saxons, the American product differing from the English in having less of dullness and more of timidity. In America there is less individuality of spoken opinion than in England, every man thinking as every other man, and afraid of every other man of his own circle, on all themes where emotions control. This analysis relates to average character, and does not overlook the fact that men of pre-eminent courage as well as genius have arisen in both countries—men who have been all the stronger for their life-long contests with the Philistinism about them.

Thirdly.—This analysis of the Salem witchcraft excitement illustrates the limitations of the human brain, and how worthless abjectly are all opinions based on, or accompanied by passion. We see the need of having a few men, even though very few, who are strong enough, expert enough, and bold enough to be before the age instead of behind it; who have the royalty and the force to lead the world up to their thought, and to stand solid and calm in the height of storms. Such men science did not have in the days of the Salem witchcraft; such men science now does have; and it is one proof of the progress of our time that they exist. How it may be in other worlds we do not know, and may never know; but this we do know, that our planet was designed for non-experts, and that those who attain to mastership in science must ever be a small fraction of society.

Joseph Green—a clergyman of Salem, who died in 1715—is one of those who may divide with Calef the honor of having opposed the delusions and murders of witchcraft, and of having aided in restoring the victims to their rights, as far as possible. Mr. Green, perhaps, more than any other one man, labored to bring about this restoration, and promote peace in the parish by rescinding the votes of excommunication against those who had been accused of witchcraft.

Francis Dane, of Andover, who opposed the delusions of witchcraft before the end of 1692, and signed memorials to the Legislature in October of that year, and to the Court about the same time, deserves to be remembered for his high and noble course, and for his fearless and outspoken denunciations of the wrongs practiced under that delusion.

His age and character were such that the accusers hardly dared to strike at him; but they accused and brought to sentence of death his grand-daughter, and caused several others of his grand-children to be imprisoned.

Fourthly—There has been, on the whole, in many respects, an improvement in our judicial dealings with insanity, trance, hysteria, and allied states.

So much has been learned of the interactions of mind and body, and especially of the influence of the emotions of fear, wonder, and expectation, in producing subjective sensations that well simulate objective sensations, that the testimony of a circle of silly girls as to what they experienced or professed to experience in seances, would count but for little against a prisoner on any charge.

Although the belief in witchcraft has not been specifically reasoned out, it has died out; and those who yet adhere to it command no hearing in court.

In recent days, insanity has judicial relations of a complex nature—the responsibility of those charged with crime, of testators, of those who make contracts of business or marriage, and of witnesses; and on the average, in all parts of our civilization, the errors of juries, if not of judges, are in the direction of mercy, of giving the supposed insane the advantage of reasonable doubt against punishment, and of reasonable doubt in favor of liberty, the exceptions being where, as in the case of Guiteau, both reason and instinct are submerged in emotion.

Hysteria, that simulates so often structural maladies, is now considered fairly and sometimes intelligently in court; experts may differ in their judgment of any special case, while agreeing as to the recognition of the disease and of its chief phenomena. Within a few years, trance, both natural and artificial, has been brought into court in France, Great Britain and America, under circumstances that made expert testimony possible and in a degree effective.

Mobs in the nineteenth century almost duplicate the mobs of the seventeenth; and when popular feeling rises to a storm for or against a prisoner on trial, the court, in this country, at least, shares in and represents the outside feeling, and executes its will quite as submissively as in Salem; and from the resulting injustice we are delivered only or mainly by the delays and respites of law, of which I shall speak hereafter. These delays, however, are of avail only on one side—the saving of the innocent; for the acquittal of the guilty which, under the plea of insanity, sometimes happens in obedience to the commands of the people, there is no remedy, except such as was urged during the trial of Guiteau, to hang the next offender, whether sane or insane, and thus by a vicarious sacrifice, to balance an injustice in one direction, by injustice in the opposite direction, and thus obtain an average of justice.

On the 5th of January, 1757, at a quarter past six in the evening, the King of France was descending from the Palace of Versailles to his carriage, followed by his attendants and surrounded by one hundred Swiss guards. A young man pushed through the guards and struck the king with a pocket-knife in his side, making a slight wound, from which he soon recovered. It is said that the modern mind cannot conceive the alarm caused in France by this trifling affair. The facts which have come down to us are not in so much detail as we could desire; but it is probable that this young man—Pierre Damiens by name—was a monomaniac of the style of Guiteau, driven insane, or excited to this special development of insanity by the political excitement of the time. It is probable, also, that he was a religious monomaniac, for he was a pious fanatic—a Jacobinist— and in his pocket were found a copy of the New Testament, and thirty gold pieces. He had no accomplices, no plan, no motives that could appeal to a sane mind, any more than had Guiteau; but it was suspected that his delusion was to force upon the king's attention the necessity for making greater efforts for the orthodox faith in France.

The treatment of the victims of the Salem witchcraft, the treatment of Guiteau at Washington, and of Bellingham in England, seem mild, sweet and polite in comparison with the treatment of this insane Damiens. From his arrest to his death—nearly three months—he was in torture; bound in chains, and frequently taken to the torture room, and there treated as the North American savages were wont to treat their victims, and with the aid of more skilful appliances for inflicting pain than Indians have. By a circuitous journey he was taken to the place of execution, guarded by a small army, all Paris ready to see the show. For half an hour he was kept waiting in view of the preparations for his murder, and in the presence of an immense assemblage—many of them delicate ladies of high rank—he was bound naked upon a table placed on a high platform. The ladies and gentry looked on with joy; those who had succeeded, through influence, in gaining good positions for seeing the spectacle, saw his right hand (the one with which he had struck the King) burned off; then pieces of flesh torn from him by red-hot pincers, and melted lead and rosin poured into his wounds; a powerful horse was attached to each of his four limbs, but it was impossible to tear him to pieces, and a request was sent to cut the muscles; but not until the request was repeated was permission given, and he did not expire until both legs and one arm had been torn from the body. His execution lasted over an hour. His body was burned, his house purchased and destroyed; and the leaders in this murder were munificently rewarded. To the two judges who pronounced sentence were given life pensions of six thousand francs a year; the lawyers, the clerks, the torturers and the executioners also had their reward.

This young man was treated as many of the women of America desire to have Guiteau treated. France applauded the punishment as America applauded the verdict in the Guiteau case; and all Europe approved, as she also approved the conviction of Guiteau. Surgeons stood by to aid the torturers, and to give them notice of approaching insensibility, as they assisted in the Salem witchcraft trials, and as they testified to the sanity of the insane Guiteau.

Judging by this case alone, one would say that there was little progress in the judicial treatment of insanity in the seventy-five years that had elapsed since the slaughter in Salem.

Taking a longer base from which to measure our angle of progress, and coming down to the latter part of the nineteenth century, we find that in trials where questions of insanity, trance, or hysteria appear, the accused have three advantages over those who were accused in Salem. First, they have counsel; secondly, they have experts to testify for them, no matter how many are against them; thirdly, they have the checks and delays of law; and of these three, the latter—the delays of law—is probably of more account than the testimony of experts or the efforts of counsel; for in the whirl of a storm counsel counts for but little, and expert skill counts for nothing.

In the Whittaker case, on the first trial, before the Court of Inquiry, at West Point, counsel was allowed, but had no influence over the court. On the subsequent court martial in this city, counsel of great ability was employed, and the defence was managed throughout with unusual skill; but in spite of it, the court martial voted at the close precisely as they would have done had they voted months before. Even if Guiteau had been well defended, it is doubtful whether any verdict in accordance with the facts could have been rendered. Time is the best and strongest ally of justice.

ADVANTAGES OF THE DELAYS OF LAW.

Fourthly.—The history of the Salem witchcraft trials is an argument for the delays of law, concerning which in recent times, men complain so much. Speedy justice is too often speedy injustice; and hanging in haste, like marrying in haste, may be the source of infinite repentance.

Had there been in Salem more delay in judicial proceedings, this book would probably have never been written; the cyclone of anger would have passed, and there would have been few or no executions; but our unfortunate ancestors there charged with witchcraft were treated as the nation desired that Cadet Whittaker and Guiteau should be treated —with prompt and thorough justice.

Arrest, prosecution, the trial, the conviction, the hanging and the burial followed in such quick, logical and conscientious succession as to have been but one event; and when the victims were suspended in the air on Witch Hill, high up in sight of the multitude, as if to defy the Prince of the power of the air in his own empire, and their bodies were thrown over the hillside and rudely buried, their neighbors felt, in their deepest consciousness, that they had done their duty, and done it promptly, and that they at last would be at peace. But here was a delusion as great as that of witchcraft itself; for all the broad diameter of this earth was not deep enough to bury these victims: a few days of speedy justice were to be followed by centuries of repentance, of sorrow and of restitution; the score of innocent victims of the necessity for protecting society who, but for their sufferings, would have died unknown, are to live forever in history and in science— immortalized by the very non-expertness of the age.

After the subsidence of the excitement, when, in default of science, the instincts of society had come to the rescue and resumed their leadership, hundreds who were in prison, convicted by the logical processes of the courts, were set free by command of the Governor of the Province; as all might have been, perchance, but for the passion for prompt punishment, which then, as now, was the war-cry of the people; had there been the delays, the appeals, the reversals and the re-examinations of our modern jurisprudence, probably not one would have suffered anything beyond imprisonment.

Cadet Whittaker—tried at West Point before a military Court of Inquiry, convicted, tried again in this city, and again convicted, though as innocent of the crime of which he was convicted as any of those who tried him, and with no evidence of guilt brought against him—has at last, within the past few days, through the delays and the checks of law, though under the cover of a technicality, received at least partial justice by the unanimous decision of the authorities at Washington.

In the case of Guiteau, a moderate delay did not secure acquittal, but this point is already secured, viz.: the diffusion through intelligent society of a knowledge of the fact that Guiteau is not only insane, but terribly insane. This is a· point that could only have been gained by the delays of law.

The delays of law give chances for new facts to appear; but that is a minor matter: my argument here is that time is needed for the subsidence of emotion, for people to recover from their anger, so that reason can come to the front. The brain heated with emotion is a non-conductor for ideas, as glass is a non-conductor for electricity; an angry man is intellectually insulated.

In the case of the Salem witchcraft trials, no new facts appeared that caused them to change their views and substitute jail delivery for murder; in the cases of Cadet Whittaker and Guiteau, no new facts have appeared, or but a few; all was known that was necessary to be known, to decide those cases justly, scientifically, humanely and in the manner best fitted for the protection of society, months ago; but as travelers over cold mountains, overtaken by blinding storms, cannot see their way, and wander about in helpless confusion and distress, knowing not whither they go, when the storm passes and the sky is clear, easily see the pathway which is just before them, so, after the storm of emotion has passed, reason is able to see the path which all along had been just beneath our feet; following which we shall be led in the direction of truth, science, justice and humanity.

In the case of Dr. Lamson, lately convicted of murder in England, the trial was short and conviction speedily gained; the interval between conviction and the time fixed for execution was very brief; and the news of the conviction and sentence were received with applause in America, as proof of the promptness of England contrasted with the slow and halting justice of America; but in less than a month both hemispheres were besieged with requests for a new trial and for the admission of evidence which—whether useful or worthless—should have been brought out on the trial, instead of after conviction and sentence; then came respites and respites, the commingled results of international courtesy and international non-expertness.

In modern times we pass through the same excitements, and in obedience to the same laws as in these ancient witch-times, the chief advantage of our own time being that we sooner correct ourselves. Now, as then, we become impatient, in hours of passion and of terror, with the restraints of law and of science. All our civilization is but veneering, which, under severe pressure, is soon rubbed off and finds us savages at heart. We cry out like children, like Indians, like Turks, and like Bedouins, for lynching, for vigilance committees, and for murder; we are hungry for injustice, but we correct ourselves more easily and more rapidly than our fathers did; the waves of popular feeling on all themes are shorter and break more quickly. Behold the history of America within the past few months; the wave of laudation of the late President; the succeeding wave of defamation of the same man; the powerful wave of excitement against Guiteau; the feeble wave of excitement in his favor; the rejoicing over the speedy verdict in the Lamson case, followed by the ransacking of hidden archives to prove him insane; the petitions for Mason and his family.

During the past year the New York Medico-Legal Society appointed a committee—of which I am one of the members—to consider the reform of the coroner's office, one of the topics discussed being the abolition of coroner's juries, which was accomplished five years ago in Massachusetts. That coroner's juries have no human worth, that their decisions have little or no influence on justice, has been well known. A partial explanation is that they receive testimony in amid the violence of whirlwinds, when the people are hot with passion, the advantage of the freshness of the facts and the accessibility of the testimony being counterbalanced many times over by the fright and anger of the witnesses.

He who should on a wager make a contract to excite the American people through the emotions, and in that way convert them to any doctrine within three months, and to a denial of the same doctrine within another three months could, if he were moderately skilful, gain his contract and win his wager.

DISAGREEMENT OF PHYSICIANS A SIGN OF PROGRESS.

In the Salem witchcraft trials there was the unanimity of opinion among experts for which the world now prays but does not often obtain; the physicians who were called in all agreed in their diagnosis; the unanimous verdict was that the symptoms of hysteria, trance, and insanity indicated witchcraft. In our days the most common complaint, next to that of the slowness of justice, is that experts are not unanimous; the disagreement of physicians is the stereotyped witticism and criticism of the hour; but this difference of opinion, this want of harmony, is the result and measure of our progress in science. Those who share these criticisms should have lived two centuries ago, when science—such as it may have been—was harmonious, and those who were summoned were all agreed on the side of delusions; through these two centuries, I hear not one opposing voice.

Mr. Herbert Spencer says in substance: The order of evolution is from the unanimity of absolute ignorance through the differences of the partially-informed to the unanimity of the wise.

In Salem there was the unanimity of absolute ignorance, the harmony of perfect non-expertness; and the prosecutions passed off as smoothly as men wished the trials of Cadet Whittaker, and Guiteau could have passed, without any obstruction on the part of scientific men; the jar, the friction, the antagonism, the repentance, and the shame came at a later date; and the managers acted—as men in a passion would act now—on the maxim of the character in the popular play, "Fatinitza," "Flog first, explanations afterwards."

When I was summoned to Washington on the Guiteau trial, one of the body of experts there suggested that it would be well if we could all meet and agree; and it was hoped by some that all could agree on the wrong side, and that that famous trial could be in that respect, as it was in many other respects, a duplicate of the Salem witchcraft trials. The expert testimony on the part of the prosecution was as harmonious as a Gothic Cathedral.

Had the trial taken place ten years ago, it probably would have been on the part of the experts as one-sided as were the Salem witchcraft trials. That it was not, that men were found to testify on the side of science, of truth, and of justice against the wishes and fury of the people, is one of the best single proofs that our country has ever offered to the world of the great progress it has made, and is making in science and in civilization.

A moral that science draws from this recital and analysis is that it is safe to be just; that only in justice can there be safety; virtue is self-preservation ; the highest justice is supreme selfishness ; the right is that which pays, the wrong is that which does not pay; non-expertness proves in time to be a speculation most unwise ; he who is dead to science buys at a falling market that may never rise ; in hours of excitement and of horror as in Salem, as in Washington, as at West Point, the best of us lose our faith in nature, and distrust the doctrine of the universality of law ; we fear that for once perchance the universe will play a trick ; that gravity or some principle quite as unbending may give way and leave us helpless, and so we steer away from the truth as though it were a siren with treacherous rocks at its feet ; we glide over it quickly as we skate over thin ice, lest it break beneath us; we mount it as we would mount an untrained horse that will throw us if it can; allowing it to hold the helm when the weather is clear and fair, we toss it aside when it is most of all needed, in the darkness or storm, and are annoyed that we are soon stranded on the shore.

What we call good and evil are but echoes of forgotten battles between the strong and the weak, in which the strong has at last conquered. At short distance injustice often prevails, while justice fights at long range, but in the end, counting its campaigns by centuries, it prevails.

The world is to learn, is learning now, that what we call mind as well as what we call matter is a part of nature and subject to nature's sovereignty; that psychology, though the youngest of the sciences, is as truly a science as astronomy, that it is indeed the scientia scientiarum before which all other sciences are to bow and veil their faces, that law reigns in the throb of passion as in the rush of a planet, and that the atoms of the cells within the brain, like the hairs without it, are all numbered.

The lesson of Salem, the lesson of West Point, the lesson of Washington is that knowledge is the friend not the enemy of society, that it is pleasant to know the truth, and wise to follow it; that what we call humanity is but science made practical, sweet and melodious; that murder under legal forms is now, as it always has been, the suicide rather than the salvation of nations; that justice is a wall about society, and every act of injustice a breach in that wall; that asylums, costly as they may be, are cheaper than scaffolds, and that in best protecting the irresponsibly insane we are best protecting ourselves.

APPENDIX A.

EXPLANATION OF THE FRONTISPIECE.

The frontispiece is designed to show the evolution of the sciences and delusions in their relation to each other. (See also pages 46-48.) A few preliminary definitions are required.

"Science is organized knowledge."

"Religion is a feeling of the supernatural and of our relations to it."

"A delusion is a belief that can be *proved* to be false." A superstition is a belief that is *felt* to be false.

The belief that Friday is an unlucky day, that the finding of a horseshoe means good luck, and in the fatality of the number thirteen at dinner, are superstitions, because, although we cannot prove them to be false, we yet feel that they are false. This feeling comes in part from the general progress of science and ordinary recognition of the domain of law in nature; but it is quite different from a scientific demonstration. Even the most ignorant of civilized beings, who know nothing of any science, yet feel that these beliefs are superstitions. A religious belief that is no longer in good form becomes a superstition.

The belief that the phenomena of trance-speaking and trance-seeing are of a supernatural origin can be "proved" to be false, since these phenomena are now brought within natural law; hence such a belief is a delusion. Before the phenomena of trance were understood, such a belief was only *felt* to be untrue; it was therefore a superstition.

Science is that which can be proved to be true. Phenomena of nature which to one race or individual are interpreted as religion, by another race are interpreted as superstitions, delusions, or sciences; whence the religion of one generation to the next generation becomes superstition, to the next, science.

Natural phenomena are constant; it is the interpretation of them which is variable, which gives rise to religions, superstitions or delusions, and the sciences.

Delusions, like the sciences, may be indefinitely specialized. This specialization is, to a limited extent, represented in the frontispiece, wherein appear the more important of the sciences, with delusions corresponding to them which the sciences have displaced.

Religion is recognized exclusively by the emotions.

Science is recognized exclusively by the intellect.

Delusions are recognized partly by the emotions and partly by the intellect.

The belief in a future life and world of spirits can neither be proved nor disproved; it is indemonstrable; it is a part of religion with which the intellect has nothing to do.

"Things that are most unknown are most proper to be deified;" religion, as religion, belongs wholly to the emotions and to the realm of the indemonstrable. Religious beliefs studied intellectually become theologies, mythologies, philosophies. If the belief in a future life and spirits could be proved scientifically, it would cease to be religion, and would become a science; it would be transferred from the realm of emotion to the realm of the intellect, and would take its place side by side with other sciences in the circle of organized knowledge of men. The demonstration of religion, therefore, would be the destruction of religion. A religion proved to be false becomes a delusion; proved to be true, a science; in either case it dies as a religion. When religion comes directly in contact with science, religion always conquers; for the emotions, in hand to hand battle, are more powerful than the intellect. Before religions can be overcome by science, they must first become superstitions—that is, felt to be false; or delusions—that is, proved to be false.

The attempt to make religion scientific—to confirm the longings of the heart by the evidence of the senses, to prove the existence of a future life and of spirits, by the phenomena of trance and the involuntary life (so-called spiritualism), is a delusion, since it can be proved to be false. It is a matter partly of the intellect, partly of the emotions. The explanation of the phenomena of trance and the involuntary life, on which the delusion of spiritualism is based, is science, a special branch of neurology and psychology, the study of the nervous system and the mind in health and disease. It is demonstrably true, and, like all the sciences, is wholly a matter of the intellect.*

* In the above definitions and analysis no reference is made to the extensive literature of the subject, for the reason that it furnishes so little aid to the inquirer. The latest work that discusses these prob-

APPENDIX A.

The great delusions of modern times, in their relation to the corresponding sciences that overcome them, are represented in the figure. (Frontispiece.)

The phenomena of the heavenly bodies were formerly referred to astrology; astronomy came and astrology passed away, its place being taken by alchemy, which delusion was to the infinitely small what astrology was to the infinitely great.

The science of chemistry came and alchemy passed away, its place being supplied by witchcraft, which was to the human body in health and disease what alchemy and astrology were to inorganic nature.

General physiology and pathology—the scientific study of the human system in health and disease—appeared, and witchcraft passed away, its place being taken by spiritualism and animal magnetism, which delusions are to the nineteenth century what witchcraft, alchemy and astrology were to the previous centuries.

lems—"Outlines of Primitive Belief," by Charles Francis Keary, M.A., F.S.A., of the British Museum (1882)—may be read with advantage, and partly for this reason that it makes clear the inadequacy of the best and most recent definitions of religion Mr. Herbert Spencer's definition, "An *a priori* Theory of the Universe," is, on one side, an advance on most of the attempts of previous thinkers; but a theory is the result of an intellectual more than of an emotional process; one may have a theory of the universe without being in any sense religious, whereas the most religious people have no theory of the universe. Mr. Matthew Arnold's definition, "Morality Touched by Emotion," is poetical rather than scientific. Were it reversed—"Emotion Touched by Morality"—it would be in the direction of the truth. The latter clause of my definition, "and of our relations to it," refers to morality.

The above definitions of delusion and superstition, and the analyses of their relations to each other, to science and to religion, are, I believe, entirely my own.

This whole subject belongs to psychology, and is to be organized in science by psychologists making use of philology and kindred sciences.

In regard to these evolutions in the forms of delusions, the following generalizations are to be noted:

First—Changes in delusions are measures of progress in the human race. Spiritualism and animal magnetism, although as truly delusions as witchcraft, alchemy or astrology, are of a milder character; they indicate in their present form more advanced modes of thinking and feeling, and the phenomena to which they refer, belonging as they do to trance and involuntary life, special departments of psychology are of a more difficult, delicate and subtle nature, than the phenomena of general pathology, which gave origin to witchcraft, or of chemistry and astronomy, which gave origin to alchemy and astrology.

The delusions of spiritualism, animal magnetism, and mind-reading, are therefore proof and results of the increasing progress of the age, and are encouraging to friends of progress; they are less cruel delusions than witchcraft; no one would die for them, nor cause others to die for them.

The delusion of animal magnetism is only possible in a scientific age, and to scientific people.

Secondly—The old delusions survive with the new, in a limited way, long after they cease to become generally believed. Even now astrologists are active in our city; and in London, I have been told, an alchemist has been seen during the last quarter of a century. With our negroes and Indians the belief in witchcraft is almost universal.

Thirdly—Delusions are not only inevitable, but they are indispensable to mankind. Our planet is ruled, is destined to be ruled by the imagination. The world can do without science—the demonstrably true; few, indeed, have any science, and those few but little; the world can even exist for a time without religion, or with almost none; the demonstrably false it will not and cannot do without. Witchcraft, bloody and terrible as it is, has probably been of supreme service to civilization, if, indeed, it be not a part of the very foundation of all our culture. Our not very far distant ancestors were not sweet and gentle, but coarse and brutal savages, who could not be led, but must be frightened, into the pathway of civilization; and for such, a belief not only in a personal and ever-present God, but in a personal and ever-present, or liable to be present, Devil, was requisite. Says Plato: "It is often necessary for the benefit of men to deceive them;" says Varro: "It is necessary that the people should be ignorant of many things that are true, and believe many things that are false;" or, if not false, at least not demonstrably true. That Christianity is one of the causes as well as one of the results of European and American civilization, is a truism in psychology; and the belief in witchcraft, until it became unfashionable and detestable, was a part of the belief in Christianity; to deny it was to be an infidel. Such was the belief in Salem in 1692; such also was the belief during the succeeding century.

APPENDIX B.

CAN THE INSANE BE LEGALLY PUNISHED?

At the present hour both continents are asking the question, whether the insane cannot be legally punished? By some it is claimed that as insanity, like other diseases, is a disease of degrees, there should be corresponding degrees of legal responsibility; that insanity as such should be no defence, but that each case of insanity leading to crime should be considered by itself in order to determine the exact degree of responsibility for the crime.

The recent and terrible increase of insanity and of crimes of violence committed by the insane in civilized countries, together with the grotesque disposition to press the insanity plea, with or without reason, in almost every case of crime in good or even medium society—makes the consideration of this question both proper and imperative; and this rising theory of gradations of legal punishment, corresponding to and accurately dovetailing with degrees of responsibility in the insane, has such a plausibility and charm for minds unused to original reasoning in solemn and complex problems of psychology, that we have to wonder that it is so rarely carried into practice, and that despite its attractiveness it has few if any consistent advocates.

On this subject the instincts of all men and of all ages speak with one voice; deeper than law, deeper than religion, deeper than philanthropy, deep as the human organism itself is the recognition of this principle that serious disease of the mind destroys legal responsibility. It is not, as many suppose or declare, the product of any sentiment or scientific theory, nor even of civilization, for it antedates sentiment and science and civilization,—laws and religions and moralities in their relations to this theme, being but formulations of the universal instinct of man; to overthrow it is to pull up human nature by the roots and cast it to the dogs. If those who hold that unwillingness to legally punish the crazy is a late evolution, a sign and result of the womanishness of the age, will take to themselves wings and fly with the speed of the swiftest bird back into the night of time, they will never come to a people sufficiently barbarized to hang the insane, knowing them to be insane, and with a clear knowledge of the nature of insanity; but through inadvertence always, through misconception, through erroneous diagnosis, supposing them to be bewitched, or supposing them to be wicked; mistaking, as is so often done by non-experts of to-day, the symptoms of mental disorder for the symptoms of vice or fanaticism or supernaturalism.

Are these universal instincts of mankind sound and true? Are they harmonious with the higher development of the race? Will they be sustained by the higher intelligence and larger experience of the future?

The following considerations and reasonings force me to answer these questions affirmatively, and to predict that, in the future as in the past, the insane who are known to be insane will not be legally punished.

1. Insanity in all its forms is a serious disease. A person who is insane is a very sick person, whatever be the type or stage of the malady from which he suffers. There is strictly no such disease as mild insanity; the phrase is indeed a contradiction; for although insanity is a disease of degrees, yet every insane person is, to a greater or less extent out of harmony with his environment, and therefore irresponsible; and has but one chance in five or ten of perfectly and permanently recovering.

By a single delusion the rich and delicate fabric of the mind may be rent in twain, beyond repair; a gun cannot burst a little, a single crack is ruin; an edifice whose foundation even at a corner gives way is reported unsafe; a steamer with but one compartment broken steers anxiously for the nearest port; if one key of an instrument be at fault we send for the tuner; a single poor player will spoil an otherwise perfect orchestra.

Many are popularly and sometimes professionally called insane who are not insane. Large numbers of victims of morbid fears and morbid impulses who in conversation and in literature pass for lunatics are not lunatics, and as a rule are never to become lunatics; sick as they may be in body or even in mind they are yet responsible and sane; thousands of sufferers from general hypochondria and monohypochondria, from neurasthenia and hysteria, remain all their lives on the border line, never crossing the border between sanity and insanity. In a series of papers entitled, "Cases of Monohypochondria and Monomania," now being published in the *New York Medical Record*, I have reported a number of these border line cases that would often pass for lunatics, but are really sane and responsible.

2. The insane do not commit the crimes of the sane, and are attracted rather than deterred by legal punishments especially of a bloody and violent character.

The loss of the power of adaptation to environment with impairment of the instinct of self-preservation, which are the essential features of insanity, render the insane incapable and indisposed to commit sane crime. This dislocation of the insane from their surroundings makes it impossible for them to work together, to organize, to combine, to plan in unison, to conspire a murder, or theft, or even an escape from an asylum; insane crimes are always solitary crimes; the lunatic has no confederate. The insane are far more likely to masturbate than to abuse women, even under abundant temptation; and in their intercourse with and relations to each other in asylums are not angered or tempted to violence by conduct or circumstances that would make sane men furious and drive them to oaths and blows if not to bloodshed.

The sane man murders those whom he hates, from whose death he expects to gain something; the insane man murders those whom he most loves—from whose death he can gain nothing—the stronger his affection for those he kills the stronger the impulse to kill them. The victims of insane murders are wives, children and friends of the murderer. Couples that live together happily, when they become insane, are more tempted to murder each other than couples that live together unhappily. A man loves himself better than any one; hence the insane are far more likely to kill themselves than to kill others. According to Dr. Dana there are in our asylums thirty suicides to one homicide.

Insanity does not so much take away our knowledge as our power; and the insane, when they commit crimes of violence, not only know right from wrong, but do the wrong solely because it is wrong; they murder because murder is a terrible and bloody deed; they murder their loved ones because such murders are more dreadful than ordinary murders; they know what they do but cannot help doing what they do.

The insane, like children and like animals, may be slightly and transiently influenced by frequent promises and givings of rewards and punishments; but no more than children, no more than animals, can they be legally punished?

Dread of going to an asylum is no doubt one exciting cause of insanity in predisposed natures, and it is doubtful whether such dread ever directly prevents a predisposed nature from becoming insane; so the sight and promise of punishment for crime attract the lunatic; and the public trials of lunatics who have committed murder, tend, as especially shown during the trial of Guiteau, to increase the number of insane murders; the insane have even committed murder for the pleasure of being hanged.

Sane people are influenced by a class of universal motives that appeal to all, civilized and uncivilized, of all lands. Among these motives are, love of life, property and physical comfort; and when we deprive or threaten to deprive any human being—whether civilized or uncivilized, of high or low social position —of life, liberty or property, we threaten them with what they know and feel to be punishment; and such threatening has an influence; and while all sane beings are not influenced to the same degree, or in the same direction—some being most sensitive to loss of esteem, one not caring to live if he cannot have the respect of his neighbors and friends, another preferring the most dreaded disease to loss of property or loss of liberty—yet some one of these punishments will influence every one; even those who desire to commit suicide, do not wish to be hanged; they wish to die, but they prefer to take their lives in their own way, and in their own time; we prefer the disgrace of suicide to the disgrace of hanging.

With the insane, on the other hand, we have no universal motive to which we can appeal if we wish to punish them; for the reason that they are out of harmony with their environment—with the world to which the sane more or less adapt themselves—the insane have no common instincts, no common feelings, no common loves, or hates, or fears; if we are to punish them we must have thousands of laws and thousands of special punishments; we must have an act that there shall be a special punishment for each form of lunacy; we must find out the special weakness of every insane offender, and punish him along the line of that weakness. One might be punished by the deprivation of his newspaper, another by confinement, another by dispossession of his property; but deprivation of money, social esteem, or even of life, with the majority of lunatics, count as trifles; consequently, we must watch them to prevent them from taking their own lives, since hanging has no debarring influence over them; constantly, also, they are impelled to take life, though they may know that if they commit murder they shall be hanged.

Then again, the insane are so weakened by their cerebral disease that they have but little prophetic and forecasting power; they see a punishment only when it is close at hand; it must constantly, specially and powerfully appeal to their senses, if they are to be influenced thereby. The prospect of hanging is so far away that—like babes—they cannot comprehend it.

There are those who suspect that the form of insanity called monomania, or reasoning mania, should be excepted from the other forms of insanity, and that those monomaniacs who commit crime should be held responsible therefor.

The reply to those who hold this view is, that monomania is the meanest kind of mania; so far from being a light and transient thing it is one of the most terrible diseases that a human being can have; its prognosis is usually dreary or doubtful, and its history one of relapse, treachery and uncertainty. I should, myself, prefer to be attacked with any other form of insanity than monomania. Melancholia sometimes perfectly recovers; likewise, though less often, raving mania; general paresis quickly affords its victim the relief of death; while the monomaniac lives, maybe for decades or for a long life; but lives not to recover but to suffer and to be the cause of severe suffering to others.

Professionally I see and have seen, many interesting cases of monomania. I have regarded them, and do regard them, not only as serious diseases, but as among the most serious of the different forms of insanity.

A man who thinks his arm is made of glass, who believes that he is emperor of the world, or a special agent of the Almighty, or in partnership with God; or who has a special divine mission to carry out in the world as the agent of Deity; who believes himself to be some great public character living or dead, or to have enormous influence with the great; or who, without reason, believes himself to be the victim of poison, or of an unfaithful companion; or believes that he is a lily or a bird, and cannot be driven out of his special delusion by the evidence of his senses, is, however clear, brilliant and powerful his intellect, however successful or useful he may be in professional life, whether in or out of an asylum, a sufferer from one of the most terrible and hopeless diseases that can afflict a human being. This disease, when it comes, usually comes to stay with its victim until they are parted by death.

Monomaniacs of this kind are usually harmless; they do not commit the crimes of the sane and but rarely those of the insane; but when they do kill themselves or others they are, to say the least, quite as irresponsible as lunatics of any other class.

As local and limited chorea—a spasm of the face or arm—is more obstinate than general chorea; as a local palsy—like writer's cramp—is harder to relieve than even a general paralysis; as a narrowly defined neuralgia, like sciatica or tic doloreux, is more agonizing and more rebellious than diffused neuralgia; so monomania, or reasoning mania, the *primäre verrücktheit*, " original craziness " of the Germans, or "crankiness" of the Americans—chronic insanity with fixed delusions—has usually a worse prognosis than more general insanity with more obstinate and varying delusions; and as a single drop of poison may defile a goblet of pure water, whereas many drops of pure water cannot purify a goblet of poison, so one insane impulse or delusion may at times, if not always, dislocate the whole nature.

3. When, therefore, the insane commit crimes of violence the presumption is enormous, if not absolute, that the crimes are directly or indirectly the result of insanity, and would not have been committed if the subjects had been sane.

This proposition is an inference from and supplementary to the preceding proposition. While it is perhaps philosophical and conceivable, that an insane man might commit a sane crime, that is, a crime which, under the same circumstances, he would have committed if he were sane; yet it is impossible in any given case to prove that this philosophic conceivability has been actually illustrated, since all experience and all the presumption are to the contrary.

When our fathers of 1692 wished to kill the witches they referred to Blackstone and Lord Hale; when American judges of to-day wish to hang the insane they refer to the McNaghton case and the grotesque decision that it called forth—non-expert lords asking non-expert questions of non-expert judges; babes answering to babes; the talk of the nursery organized

APPENDIX B.

into precedents for murder in both hemispheres. But in England as in this country the McNaghton case is authoritative only where the insane murderer has so few friends and so little money that it is easier to hang than to acquit him. If ever a man knew what he was about, certainly McLean knew what he was about, what he wished to accomplish and why—knew right from wrong in the abstract and in the concrete—when he fired his pistol at the queen, and by the McNaghton precedent, he should have been executed; but the will of the people and the instincts of justice, fortunately, were stronger than the logic of the courts. In our own country insane murderers are very rarely hanged; the charges of judges, based on the McNaghton case, which ought to punish nearly all lunatics, having, as a rule, no influence with juries. Guiteau is the only prominent insane murderer of recent years that has been convicted and condemned to the scaffold. Even during and since his trial a number of other murderers, in different parts of the country, with far less evidence of insanity than he, have been acquitted.

It is not often that I find myself in accord with lawyers on those questions where law and psychology come in conflict. I am, therefore, surprised to find that one of the most eminent criminal lawyers of England, Mr. Serjeant Ballantine, in his just published work, "Some Experiences of a Barrister's Life," expresses on pp. 205, *et. seq.*, opinions almost, if not quite as positive as my own. Speaking of the questions presented by the lords to the judges on the McNaghton case, and of the replies of the judges, he says, that the proceeding was "very singular, had no precedent, and,

CAN THE INSANE BE LEGALLY PUNISHED?

fortunately, has never been repeated;" * * "such a proceeding was extra-judicial," * * " what was asked of them was to make a law in anticipation of facts that might hereafter arise," * * " they have not greatly assisted the administration of justice." Yet further he says: " I cannot think that where an insane delusion is clearly proved (although numerous facts may be brought forward to show that the lunatic distinguished, up to the time of the offence, the difference between right and wrong), the deluded one ought to be consigned to the gallows. The gout that has taken possession of a man's toe suddenly leaps to his heart. When a man believes himself to be the Saviour, how is it possible for human skill to tell what thought or opinion is likely to control any act of his life? The law must yield to the dispensation of Providence, however much prejudice and passion may seek to sway its administration."

Throughout this treatise and elsewhere I have used the word crime in connection with the acts of the insane, but strictly the term cannot be used in such a relation. In those countries whence we have derived nearly all our scientific knowledge of insanity, a lunatic is no more capable of committing a crime than is an infant. In France the law reads: "There can be no crime nor offence if the accused was in a state of madness at the time of the act."

The German penal code reads thus: " An act is not punishable when the person at the time of doing it was in a state of unconsciousness, or of disease of mind, by which a free determination of the will was excluded."

If we wish to hang a baby we must swear that it is not a baby but a dwarf; if we wish to hang a lunatic we must swear that he is not a lunatic but a villain, with the symptoms of vice.

Those who would further study this subject would do wisely to read William H. Seward's defence of the insane negro Freeman, in "Great Speeches by Great Lawyers," pp. 149 *et. seq.* Erskine's defence of Hadfield and Esquirol's remarkable chapter on monomania.

4. The insane as well as the sane are entitled to the benefit of doubt or the presumption of innocence.

In any case of crime committed by an insane person, it is impossible to prove beyond doubt that the crime is not a direct or indirect result of the insanity; the presumption is, and always must be, the other way.

A lunatic is legally innocent of the offence which is the result of his lunacy. The presumption is and has always been that these offences of lunatics are the results of the lunacy, and it is impossible to prove the contrary, to say the least, beyond a reasonable doubt, to which he is entitled. To prove the contrary in any case of insanity would indeed require the highest order of superhuman power. A lunatic cannot therefore be convicted of a crime. The instincts and customs of mankind are, therefore, justified by logic and psychology.

In the future as in the past, the doctrine will be that a lunatic can commit no crime, that in reference to crimes all insanity is legal insanity, that punishability—*strafbarkeit* of the Germans—belongs only to the sane, and when in deference to the desire of the people, the court wishes to punish a lunatic it must, as in the case of Guiteau, obtain testimony, which is always in the market, that the symptoms of insanity are the symptoms of sanity, or that the man who is medically insane is not legally so; and this trick will be successfully attempted only in the case of lunatics who have no money and no lawyers. We are more likely to give up our homes and live in wigwams, or to cast off our garments and walk naked through the earth, than to systematically punish the insane.

In the future as in the past it will be held that a lunatic may be capable of making wills and contracts and of giving testimony in court, even if not responsible for any offence he may have committed or might commit; in other words, the benefit of all doubt, in dealing with the insane as with the sane, will be appropriated not by the State but by the accused.

The psychology of the future will not admit the plea of insanity, except for those who are really insane, who are seriously sick in mind and who manifest their insanity by decline in the activity of the instinct of self-preservation and in the power of adapting themselves to environment, by important moral decline, or by lack of rememberable consciousness; simple eccentricity, or hypochondria, or hysteria, or morbid impulses, or morbid fears, will not be regarded as diagnostic of insanity.

The opinions of the insane themselves have been lately sought by inquirers on this question of punishability. Some of the insane declare that they are influenced by fear of punishment, that they murder because they cannot be hanged; that they would

APPENDIX B.

have abstained from their crimes, had they not expected immunity. With the people, and even with some psychologists, these insane dreams or whims are felt to be satisfactory. The answer is not far away; lunatics are not authorities in lunacy, and their opinions on this problem of their own punishability, are of as little worth as their opinions of their own sanity. The statements of insane patients in regard to the question of their sanity or insanity, do not have, and can never have scientific or practical value; if they chance to be right, it is only by chance; their diagnosis does not even aid us in our diagnosis—saying is not knowing, and knowing is not doing; the insane do not know what they will or will not do, under their attacks of insane delusions or impulses. It were wiser to appeal to a nursery than to an asylum for a final solution of problems in psychology. On this point the actions of lunatics are more instructive than their statements. Among the several hundred thousand inmates of European and American asylums, only motiveless murders are committed, and then with comparative infrequency, considering their opportunities and provocations, and the fact known to all of them that they will not be punished for anything they may do. Patients who have simply morbid fears, or morbid impulses, are not necessarily or usually insane; and such persons, like the sane generally, are responsible and punishable. Morbid fears, the absurdity of which is recognized by the sufferer, and morbid impulses, as to kill one's self or others, that can be perfectly and permanently controlled, are not symptoms of insanity, although they have almost universally been so regarded. These morbid fears—as fear of society, of being alone, of traveling alone, of crossing a ferry, of meeting drunken persons, of open squares, of closed rooms, of lightning, of storms, of diseases—are very common with my nervous patients, and morbid impulses also ; and only in a fraction of cases do they lead to positive insanity.* The distinction between morbid impulses and morbid fancyings, or dread of impulse, cannot, as it seems to me, be maintained ; the only difference between the impulses of the sane and the insane being one of controllability and degree.

The hanging of the insane would have then two effects. It would increase insanity, and it would also increase the crimes of violence committed by the insane. It is a law of psychology as universal as gravity, or centrifugal and centripetal forces, that we are drawn towards, as well as repelled, by what we greatly dread. In sane and healthy natures, the repulsion more than counterbalances the attraction ; in disease, the attraction more than counterbalances the repulsion.

Dreams are the delusions of the sane ; insanity is a waking dream ; its delusions and impulses being as uncontrollable as nightmares and nocturnal visions. If, on retiring for the night, we should be threatened with death if we dreamed of murder, our dreams would be rendered not less but more murderous thereby. The moth rushes to its death into the candle-flame ; so terrified is the bird by the serpent's eye that it is gradually drawn toward its fangs ; the screech of the elephant so alarms the untrained horse

* In my work on Neurasthenia (Nervous Exhaustion) I have described these morbid fears more in detail than is here possible.

that it cannot escape: the slow crocodile catches the swift antelope through the fascination of fear; even the dull toad is paralyzed by the sight of fire, and is burned through its very dread of burning; and the murderer returns to the scene of his bloody deeds, though he thus increases the chances of detection. The sight or tidings of horrid crime or of horrid punishment, through the law of mental contagion, so acts on natures organized for insanity and tilted on its edge as to throw them completely over, and cause them to repeat the crime, at the risk of the punishment. Milder and less imposing procedures, that act less violently on the emotions,—such as flogging, or confinement in jail or asylum—have the deterring, without the attractive force of punishment.

Says Mr. Seward, in his defence of Freeman, "the execution of a madman is murder." * * "I am not the prisoner's lawyer, * * I am the lawyer for society." Confinement for life in an asylum under the protection, if need be, of special laws, to prevent premature liberation, will protect society against the lunatic, and the lunatic against society.

Thus it will be seen that on this question of punishing the insane, the customs and instincts of mankind, the teachings of psychology, the practice of the courts, and the protection of society,—science, justice and humanity are in harmony.

PETITION FOR A STAY OF PROCEEDINGS IN THE CASE OF GUITEAU.

The following petition was prepared for circulation in the profession. It was not expected that a large number of signatures would be secured ; but the publication of it gave an opportunity for those who were in accord with its sentiments, to make a formal protest on the side of justice, and to save themselves the reproach of the future. Many physicians who regarded Guiteau as insane, yet held to the opinion that there might be a partial responsibility in some forms of insanity. But at least a dozen of the best authorities in the country had publicly expressed the opinion that Guiteau was insane and should not be hanged.

The settled opinion of the future will be that the death of President Garfield was a horrible accident, as though he had been crushed in a railway collision, or suffocated in a burning theatre, or suddenly stabbed while walking the wards of an asylum.

To the President of the United States of America :

WE, the undersigned, Citizens of the United States, and Members of the Medical Profession, respectfully and urgently petition, in the name of Psychological Science, for a Stay of Execution in the case of CHARLES J. GUITEAU.

Our petition is based on the following facts:

First.—For more than twenty years Guiteau has been hopelessly insane. This is the concurrent verdict of our leading authorities— those whose writings, researches, and opinions on diseases of the nervous system exert the greatest influence in this country and in other countries. These authorities have frequently and publicly expressed this opinion in the most positive manner, during and since the trial, before scientific bodies, and in scientific journals specially devoted to medico legal and psychological questions.

Secondly.—Under a right management of the case these opinions could have been formally brought before the Court, and would have radically changed the character and probably also the issue of the trial.

APPENDIX B.

Third.—The instincts and the customs of all civilized nations are opposed to the hanging of the insane. Even since the case of Guiteau has been before the world, the manner of dealing with insane murderers has been illustrated both in America and in Europe. In this country inmates of asylums who chance to commit murder, are not tried nor even arrested. In England, the lunatic McLean was at once acquitted and sent to an asylum, although the published evidence of his insanity is not so abundant as the evidence of the insanity of Guiteau.

Years since, the insanity of Guiteau was recognized by some of his relatives, and formal efforts were made to send him to an asylum, as an incurable and dangerous lunatic. One medical certificate (that of the family physician) was ready, and but for a complication of accidents, the other would have been obtained. We hold that during these twenty years no asylum in the world would have refused admission to Guiteau, and in all probability none would have discharged him. We hold that the insane out of asylums as well as in asylums, are entitled to the protection of that law which declares that no lunatic can commit a ciime.

If this petition for a stay of proceedings should be granted, we would further petition for the appointment of a commission composed of our best recognized authorities who did not testify at the trial, to examine into the mental condition of Guiteau, and report thereon.

In Germany and in France—countries which have led the world in the scientific study of insanity—it has long been the custom to appoint such committees of experts in cases where the plea of insanity has been entered, and receive their reports *before* the trial. If this course had been pursued in the case of Guiteau, this country would have been spared the humiliation and disgrace of a protracted trial of a lunatic.

The following letter appeared in the *Boston Medical and Surgical Journal*, June 1, 1882. It was in reply to an editorial of ability and intelligence, in which the positions taken were that Guiteau was insane, that he should not have been tried, but that, inasmuch as the contrary opinion had prevailed in Court, it would be better to let the law take its course:

MR. EDITOR:—Your editorial on Guiteau, and the petition for a stay of proceedings, in your issue of May 18th, was written so carefully, and contains so much of truth, that, by your permission, I will briefly reply to one or two statements with which I cannot agree.

(1.) You say that, inasmuch as Guiteau has been unjustly condemned, society should now have the benefit of the doubt ; that the trial which you properly characterize as disgraceful, and a verdict which—from your point of view and mine—is unjust, should be supplemented by hanging; in a word, that one injustice can be corrected by another injustice ; that although it was wrong to even try Guiteau, it is right to hang him.

The benefit of a doubt belongs to the accused, not only before and during the trial, but after a verdict, and after a succession of verdicts, and up to and after execution ; through all time, hanged or unhanged, Guiteau must be held to be presumably insane.

It was by this benefit of doubt that Cadet Whittaker—with whose case I was professionally connected—lately obtained in Washington, after two unjust verdicts, contrary to the evidence, substantial though tardy vindication.

In the case of Guiteau the interference of the profession is needed now more than ever before. Says your neighbor Lowell :

" Then to side with truth is noble, when you share its wretched crust."

Of the large number of authorities on the nervous system who have lately published the opinion that Guiteau was insane, only a fraction testified on the trial. Casting aside all the opinions in favor of his

APPENDIX B.

insanity presented on the trial, and all others that have since been published by others and myself as of no value, *there has appeared in your journal alone* adequate quality and sufficient quantity of evidence for the defence to have saved the assassin from the scaffold, had the case been only one of ordinary interest.

No lunatic ever hauled before a court in this country, or any other country, so far as I can learn, has ever obtained so much expert testimony of a high order in favor of his insanity as has Guiteau. In making this statement I count my own opinions for naught. If the result of this protest of the profession shall be the substitution of permanent confinement for life for the halter, practical justice will have been gained. Whether the experts that the President should appoint should agree or not is of no moment.

(2.) You say that Guiteau, though insane, is less insane than the evidence seemed to make him.

Some of the worst diseases have no pathology; the type of insanity which, as we all agree, Guiteau represents, has no important physical symptoms that the senses can discover. What cannot be seen, or felt, or heard, the non-expert and non-disciplined mind doubts or denies. A post-mortem examination will probably find nothing in Guiteau's brain to account for his insanity, and yet his craziness is of a terrible and incurable character. It took eight generations of clergymen to make an Emerson; it took, perhaps, half as many generations of philosophers and scholars to make a Darwin; it took, we know not how many generations of fanaticism and degeneration to produce, by the law of the escape of the weakest, a Guiteau; but in this waste product, cast off in the evolution of the race, insanity is organized as firmly as Darwin's science or Emerson's poetry.

Although insanity is a disease of degree, yet such a disease as *mild* insanity has never existed, can never exist, and the popular belief in its existence is as truly a mistake as the belief in witchcraft.

(3.) You say that "the assassin has little claim upon the interest or sympathy of the community."

This is quite true; it is quite as true of nearly all assassins and of

CAN THE INSANE BE LEGALLY PUNISHED?

thousands upon thousands of our fellow beings, sane and insane. Shall we, therefore, slaughter them all to-morrow? Insanity is always a disgusting disease; our first impulse in dealing with lunatics is to knock them down. What is done to Guiteau is of no account; what we do, or allow to be done to him is of all account. Guiteau is as ready for the scaffold as for his breakfast; but is it, therefore, all the same whether we hang him or feed him?

Psychology does not plead for Guiteau, but for his would-be murderers. The sufferers from the Salem witchcraft excitement in 1692 were not the twenty victims, but the survivors and their descendants and descendants' descendants, to this hour.

(4.) It may be said, it has been said, that America is the non-expert's land; that the mob will have its way, and that the profession can do little; but for this reason it should do that little. Mobs are not authorities in psychology, and are not to be cruelly censured for their ignorance or even for their passion; but we are to be censured and shall be censured by posterity,—the verdict of which is as sure as the future—for not at least trying to save the mob from itself. Experts are the guardians of non-experts, and in a degree responsible for them, like parents for children.

The conduct of our profession in its relation to these popular delusions is a line of darkness and of blood in our history for more than two hundred years. In Salem it was a physician who mistook the symptoms of nervous disease for the symptoms of possession of the devil, and so started and stimulated the witchcraft trials and executions; in Auburn a physician testified that the demented Freeman, whom Seward defended, was responsible; at West Point it was a physician who declared that the unconscious cadet, Whittaker, was feigning and conscious; in Washington, what you call "those disgraceful three months," were slightly redeemed by the fact that, for almost the first time in our history, a few authorities in psychology testified against the unanimous opposition of the nation.

If, as has been said of Salem, "the pathway through the court must lead to gallows hill;" if Guiteau is to pay on the scaffold the penalty

APPENDIX B.

of his countrymen's non-expertness in psychology; if the principle of expiation is to be transferred from theology to law, and the sins of our people in so often acquitting the sane on the insanity plea are so numerous that only the blood of a lunatic can wash them away; if on this one has the lot fallen to be the last important insane murderer to be himself murdered, as the twenty victims of the witchcraft excitement were about the last who suffered for the imaginary crime, then it will be something to be able to say for this time and for all time, that there were a few at least who, from the first, and with all the force of their natures, protested against the trial, and that up to the last moment the representatives of American psychology, to whom alone the question belongs, were not unanimously consenting to that colossal crime.

Yours truly,
GEORGE M. BEARD.

NEW YORK, *May* 20.

www.ingramcontent.com/pod-product-compliance
Lightning Source LLC
Chambersburg PA
CBHW031336160426
43196CB00007B/705